Writing In The World Today:
A Contemporary Anthology

Dr. Kelly Buffone

DEDICATION

I dedicate this book to all those that impressed upon me their soul and wit
and compassion. You know who you are. I dedicate this book to all the
great teachers that took the extra time just because they cared. You know
who you are. I dedicate this book to all the dreamers, visionaries, life livers,
lovers, sinners, patriots, and warriors. You know who you are. Lastly, I
dedicate this book to my loved ones. My beautiful family, who has been
there all the way. Through the light and darkness. I am forever in your debt.
You know who you are.

CONTENTS

i Wanna

I wanna write with abandon, I wanna become the rain, I wanna lift the heavens, and drench the poor with golden showers

I wanna do soo much, but I have the body of a retired turtle. Laziness stuck inside the thin film between skin and muscle

I wanna tell everyone to lighten the fuck up, I wanna enlighten the sidewalks, bury the past, refresh the tingling mountains, spark a new generation, flower the powers that be, get old like wine, and sit back on steamy days of malaise and sip on here and there, contemplate rotating stars, drinking landscapes and devouring memories.

I wanna be sweet jazz, clarinet melodies dancing on rooftops, I wanna be horns from harlem back roads, shifting the bricks that bleak black solitude. I wanna sing with ghosts, play blues for the dead earth, revive lost hopes and cream the dreams with strawberry toppings, snow sweetness on everything, sadness made of molasses, I wanna cuddle the huddled masses, inside the dome   of   classless   classes

I wanna relax, sit back, kiss myself when she gets near, pat the howling cat on the back and tell her she can have that shadow she desires. I wanna be fleeting breath, leave a happy nest and tweet with the motherlode of mankind. What is mankind? What kind of man is this kind man of mankind? I wanna kick mankind in the balls, shout at the shouting spleen, play drums on his ribs, and make guitar strings out of his eyelashes, orchestrate a new kind of mankind, like Ludwig, and bring back the hollow flute.

I wanna let her know she doesn't have to try so hard, struttin with big bad badass sass, eyes smoky from dark thoughts, boots stained with regret, face toiled with gin, wobbly toes, and smeared chin.

I wanna let the whole world know that we are just children and nobody knows nobody from nothing and nowhere. We will be forgiven, it is stamped on us at the beginnin, birthright from upright, we shall take flight on the wings of nightless night.

Someday I'll bee there on your shoulder feelin you feelin me, light breeze, with gentle ease, you'll look up and see, something like a honey bee, not afraid to flee, know the eternal kiss is there when you feel that sweet sting.

THE PRAYER

There he lay in bed, two thirty in the morning. The dark passing shadows of the headlights drifting into the room. His wife asleep beside him. His son snoring his little breathless snore in the crib at the foot of the bed. The dog asleep in the kennel next to the bed. Everyone asleep but him. Usually this would bother him. But he felt a sudden peace surge through him. He liked the quiet. He was nowhere near sleep. He was wide awake. He thought of the angry biker from earlier that morning. How he spat at the window with his harsh words. All the while ramming his middle finger in the air. 'You came this close to me!' The angry biker roared, bringing his index finger and thumb inches apart. 'You could've killed me asshole!' He remembered how he did almost kill the poor biker, rushing through traffic, because he was late, as usual, but wasn't apologetic about it till now. At the time of the incident he was obstinate, and used a few choice words himself to fling at the man. Suddenly an image of the man's face became crystal clear to him. He had a forlorn look. There was an abundance of pain behind those angry words. Suddenly he could see that precisely as if the facade of his face had been lifted and a bird's eye view of a burdened heart was unveiled.

He closed his eyes. Clasped his hands. And these words trembled his lips silently...

Dear Lord,

May All seen and unseen experience

The peace inherent.

Images of the cosmos spilled over his consciousness. He could feel his chest expand. He felt as though he had enough in him to heal the whole universe. He saw a giant heart suspended in the vast sky. Large shafts of light beamed forth, to the four corners of the earth. People were showered with this light. He continued his prayer...

My all see the truth about struggle.

That it is nothing more than the flowering

Of their very own existence. That it is

Nothing to be avoided. Nothing to be feared.

But rather, to be embraced and suffused in their own

Experience of becoming eternal.

He felt his body lose all sense of gravity. It was the lightest he ever felt. He could perceive a sense of levitation in his limbs. Every molecule radiated this levity. He continued his prayer...

May all know that nothing is to be taken seriously.

Especially death.

That everything that happens is a direct

Commandment of the universe itself.

All one needs to do is trust this

And let go.

He could see people waking up the next morning anew. He envisioned his little prayer floating out there, gliding across continents, stretching out its song across the plains, the seas, the mountain ranges, whispering its meaning in every sleeping ear, and tap dancing along the stars, in clear view for all to see.

May all know that you intended this to be enjoyed

Not suffered through.

May all know that they need not worry about knowing.

That everything has been accounted for.

That all have what they need whenever it is necessary.

That all one needs to do is end the search.

And look within.

He heard his heart pump softly under the covers. His breath was fluid. His mind blank. Everything was automatic. He was a receiver, an antennae, and he knew not where these words came from, and he didn't care. He had a vision of a large throng of faces from all different backgrounds and they were all smiling. In the middle of this sea of smiles was the biker. He wore the biggest smile of them all.

Dr. Kelly Buffone

Dr. Kelly Buffone

Free Fall

It was something like a free fall then my eyes opened. The first thing I saw, after slowly adjusting, was a large brown door, that looked to be made of the strongest oak. After a time, I gathered it was a door leading into a private office. There was no name on the door. Adjacent to the door was a large glass window with what looked to be, drawn Venetian blinds. I heard faint sounds of typing, telephones ringing, and the clicks of what could only be the unmistakable sounds of high-heeled shoes. I looked around. There were long rows of broad desks lining the middle of the large room, with people sitting behind computer screens and stacks upon stacks of folders, envelopes, and other miscellaneous paperwork scattered about making the impression that I was back in my high school office. It even faintly smelled like my high school office, that irrefutable odor that consisted of a mixture of generic perfume and weathered carpeting. How did I get here? To attempt to convey the notion that I was flummoxed, would be an act of pure foolishness. Because I couldn't even come close to describing the feeling of blinding bewilderment I felt sitting in that chair, facing that large Oak door, with that sound of typing, and the sight of shadowy faces that never bore an expression... and I haven't even mentioned the lighting. If you could picture a room bathed in aqua-green that illuminated only the faintest figures passing to and fro across the pathways of my sight and into large dark hallways that seemed to lead to nowhere, almost swallowing its visitors, then you may be able to imagine what visions befell me. The floor was some sort of yellow-orange carpeting, so thin that to call it carpet may be an insult. A tall thin woman peeked over at me behind the first desk in the long procession. She wore large spectacles that seemed plastered to her face. Her eyes were magnified by the thick lens leaving an impression that she was part sea turtle. Was she looking at me? I couldn't tell. Then she moved her lips. Or at least I thought she did. Words came out.

"He'll be with you in just a minute," she said, as if I had been peering around impatiently. Maybe I was.

"Thank you," I said, not sure that I really had spoken. She disappeared behind a mound of paperwork. I remember those first words I uttered felt so strange because the sound of my voice wasn't the sound I usually heard when speaking. The tone actually reminded me of the impression my voice made when I heard its recorded version, which always felt so foreign to me. "Is that what I really sound like?" were not uncommon reactions when I would play back my voicemail or hear myself on a videotape.

Then he spoke. Almost through the door. Rising through my toes. Through my head.

"Come in," the voice beckoned. I looked around. I felt a slight tremor at first, but almost immediately, after the door became slightly ajar, seemingly on its own, a sense of calm came over me, and it all came back. The car, the dare, the party, the gamble, the idiocy of it all came rushing back. I walked into the office.

It was a small office. Book shelves flanked the tiny desk that separated me from him. I remember there not being any titles on the spines of the books. Bare white multiplied along the shelves. The room was very well lit. The carpet was thicker than the outer office and a shade of forest green. The wallpaper was beige colored. A stool sat in front of the desk. It was a glaring white leather seat I remember. Behind the desk, writing something down rapidly, with nothing but a bald head greeting me, was what looked to be a man in his late forties, stocky, and paunchy. He was wearing a suit vest of navy blue over a white collared shirt with rolled up sleeves and a mud colored tie. Without raising his head he told me to have a seat. He stood up, still not facing me, and placed what he was writing into a file cabinet then sat back down. He pulled out a thin white leather container or box from under the desk, about the width and length of a shoe box, and placed it firmly in front him. He looked up at me with dark brown eyes that seemed out of place in his head, like two placid planets that fell into the wrong orbit.

"You know why you're here right?" he said, with a broad smile, that seemed sincere in wanting me to be comfortable.

"I know I'm dead, but something tells me this isn't heaven."

He laughed a small laugh. "Heaven," he said shaking his head with another small laugh, "I haven't heard that word in awhile. I sometimes forget how imaginative that level is."

"Level?" I queried. .

He came out of his revery quickly and straightened up leaning forward. "You see this Sam," he said, as if he was an old friend of mine, referring to the white leather box. "This is going to explain everything."

"What's inside it?" I said motioning to grab it.

He placed his hand on it, preventing me from taking it. "It will explain everything, just don't open it in front of anyone. It's very important that you open it in private."

I took my hand off of it.

"Now, I am going to get you started with some of the basic information about what's going on," he said, getting down to business. "Then it's all up to you."

"I don't understand."

"You will eventually, just pay attention. After I give you you're password you are to walk outside and you will see a giant Elm tree in the middle of the West end of Canary Park. You are to go and sit under this tree. This is where you will open your box." He stood up and rummaged through the books with no names on the bookshelf until he came to one that seemed to satisfy him. He pulled it out and on the cover was my full name in gold letters. He flipped though the pages and I could see no writing at all until he came to about three-quarters of the way into the book where there was one word imprinted in black letters on the top left corner of the white page. It was too small a font to make out the word from my end. "Hmm..." he murmured, "black.... that's interesting."

"What does that mean? What do you mean interesting?" I said hectically.

"Don't worry about it. You know, you worry too much Sam," he said with such an air of familiarity that I was warmly rendered speechless. I actually felt warm underneath my skin, like I never felt warm before.

"What does it say?" I asked.

He began to write it down, acting like my

question was meaningless. He folded a small piece of paper and handed it to me. "Don't lose this. This will get you outside." He closed his eyes suddenly and placed his hand on his forehead. "Miss Werther," he said, talking not to me. "We're ready for a runner," he spoke again. He opened his eyes and looked at me with a fatherly smile. There was a knock at the door. He turned back to me. "Well Sam, this is it. Good luck," he said with finality and resumed some writing that he seemed to have been working on earlier. I stood up, walked to the door, feeling warm as ever. Was all this real? Am I sleeping? Am I going to wake up anytime soon?

"Aren't you forgetting something Sam?" I heard behind me. I turned around and shambled towards the desk. I picked up the box, walked back to the door slowly and then turned back around.

"Are you God?"

He stopped writing, smiled real big then said, "What do you think?"

I smiled.

"I knew it. Somehow I knew it," I said after a moment.

"Sorry to disappoint you."

"No. Not disappointed at all... just a little surprised... and yet, not surprised at all."

He broadened his smile and seemed to be scrutinizing me for a few seconds. I concluded that he might have been surprised himself.

"Do you have a name?" I asked.

"Why do you want to know my name?" he said with a light laugh. "We'll never meet again."

"I don't know why," I said. "Please?"

He stood up with a grin on his face and extended his hand. "Roland. Roland Barmashian." I shook his hand which was the warmest and softest hand I have ever felt. Baby bottoms wouldn't stand a chance with the softness of his hand.

"So, this is it then?" I said.

He pointed to the white leather package in my hand then crossed back to the desk. I walked out of the office, eager as ever to get to that Elm tree.

◆

I closed the door to Roland's office and standing there waiting for me was a fire-red-haired boy that couldn't have been more than fourteen years old. He possessed the kind of demeanor and playful mischievousness that you would imagine Huckleberry Finn to have. He looked, at close range, almost exactly like the illustrations of E.W. Kemble. He wore denim overalls, no shoes, and a coffee colored undershirt. He bounced around and moved with unflinching energy. I couldn't have asked for a better runner. As soon as I heard his voice I knew everything was full steam ahead.

"Hey Sam, I'm Chuck," he said, rushing towards me. The tiny freckles on his face danced like fireflies.

Chuck had the kind of smile you wanted to see after a long day of toil and drudgery. It almost covered his entire face, which seemed perfectly round. The type of smile that belonged in front of campfires, at the entrance of heaven, the kind you wished nurses and cops had. "Oh boy, I wish I could go back to that desk and all those questions rumbling in my head. You must be buzzing like a bumblebee. Are you ready for the tunnel?" he said, bouncing, jumping, shoulders oscillating.

"Um... I think so... what tunnel?" I said.

He grabbed my hand with lightning quickness and led the way. "You'll see. Everything is gonna be alright, don't you worry your pretty little head Sam."

Somehow everybody knew my name. Somehow

it didn't faze me at all. Chuck dragged me past the rows of desks and the women behind them, with spectacles and steadfast hands, typing away and answering phone calls. I noticed the lighting had changed. Everything was well lit, like in Roland's office. "You think you could explain this tunnel thing for me Chuck?" I pleaded. He paid me no attention. It was full steam ahead.

"To the outside!" Chuck yelled at a someone behind a circular table that sat next to an entrance of some sort. We stopped momentarily. The entrance was like a living shadow. Dark and ominous. There was no door, but then again there was one as well. And the darkness seemed to be pulsating, as though it were a living entity. If pitch black had a physical presence then this entrance was its living embodiment. It was designed in a sense that living, breathing, dark smoke had the potential for being contained. A wave of cold ascended my spinal cord. .

"Name?" the man spoke sitting behind the circular desk. He was a thin man, with icy blue eyes, and a scornful mouth. He looked to be in his late twenties, maybe early thirties. He was unshaved, unmoved, and in his voice I detected a tediousness that shrouded his duty, almost like he had been punished for some transgression and his verdict was to sit at this post for an indeterminate amount of time. I felt chilly. I rubbed my free hand against the back of my arm and shoulder. The man wore a pumpkin-orange colored dress shirt with a black tie, that sloppily rested on his chest. His dark hair seemed to be wet, or moist rather, falling in tiny sharp strands across his forehead.

"You know dam well what that young man's name is Chandler," a female voice hollered from the depths of typing, ringing, and filing behind us. It sounded like the same woman from earlier. Chuck looked at me with a smile that seemed to say, "We get this kind of thing all the time." Chandler seemed to register the comment. He rolled his eyes, licked his lips, straightened up slightly, then looked up at me with a sardonic smile. "Good luck," he said as he stretched his arm out to me with what looked like a piece of aluminum foil between his thumb and index finger. Chuck snagged the shiny thing out of Chandler's hand then grabbed the inside of my arm and took me aside. He looked up at me with a solemn expression. His lips pursed together in a determined manner and he took the foil, or whatever it was, and tore it into two small squares the size of a stamp. He told me to bend down slightly. I did, in a withering silence. He placed the two squares behind my ear lobes.

"What the hell is that?" I squealed. He paid me no mind. I felt a slight coolness on my earlobes and went to touch them. Chuck slapped at my hands.

"Don't."

"Chuck, please tell me what the hell is going on? Am I going outside or not?"

"Of course you are goofy," he replied, with his signature smile replenished on his face. "Now just hold off on the questions Sam, okay? You got your package, and that is all you need to focus on for now.

Just shush your brain for a few and let me go over some details."

"Absolutely." I motioned with my hands in a zipping movement across my lips.

"That's a good boy." He stopped for a moment then placed his left hand on my shoulder. "Here's what you're gonna do." He tilted his head toward the dark entrance. "You see that?"

I nodded.

"That there is the tunnel to the outside."

I put my finger up. He shook his head and made some don't-you-dare sounds. "No questions. You're always questioning things."

The way he said it sounded incredibly familiar I remembered thinking.

"Now relax. You're gonna walk through that tunnel, and you may feel afraid at first, but everything is gonna be alright." I had a feeling Chuck was going to tell me that. From the moment I opened my eyes sitting in that chair before Roland's office, barely making out the dark patches beyond beehive hairdos, something deeply rooted in me told me that I would have to, in some way or form, deal with what was beyond that colorless enigma.

I got a flash of Chandler's creepy smile. Apparently he could hear everything Chuck was saying and reveling in some personal secret, his lips formed in an arrogant curl. "At the right time you're gonna walk out of that tunnel and never turn back."

"Wait a minute, your not coming with me?" I couldn't help myself.

"No Sam, you have walk alone," Chuck said, knowing full well what was happening inside me, and abided with my broken silence.

"Why?" I said breathlessly. I felt iciness all over me. Chuck just smiled at me. "I thought you were my runner? What do you mean, at the right time?" I asked after a moment.

"We depend on time around here too, Sam," he said, with a beaming smile. "But time depends more on us that it did before."

"But how will I know what to do, where to go? I don't know what tree to sit under? I don't understand, why does it have to be like this? Can't someone come with me? Why can't you come with me? Doesn't anybody care how confusing this whole process is?

Maybe we should go back to Roland and check with him about all this?"

Chuck squeezed my shoulder. "Sam, don't worry about it. I know you are confused and I know you got a million question marks swimming in your head. But you have to trust me. You just hold on to that white box, and when the right time comes you will open it and all will be crystal. It's gonna be beautiful, I promise you. Everything will be just perfect."

"Why did he say 'good luck'?"

"Cause you're gonna need it chum," Chandler's voice sailed over Chuck's shoulder. His face contorted in a malicious angle, his eyes soaked in some kind of hope for defeat I perceived. That did it for me. I was now trembling. I felt that everything was adding up to one big crushing blow. I felt rising up in me something more prominent than fear. It was downright hysteria coursing my limbs. I became weary and skeptical about everything. I even looked at Chuck differently.

"One more peep out of you horse-face and I'm gonna make you eat that tie," Chuck said, without turning around to face Chandler. His eyes remained locked on mine. Chandler rolled his eyes, but I think the comment achieved the desired effect. I could tell by the way Chuck's mouth was positioned that he was discouraged to see me adopt a sullen posture so quickly.

"Don't you pay any attention to him, to anybody, including your own self," Chuck spoke softly, his eyes glittering. "Most of all yourself. There's nothing more

Writing In The World Today

deceptive than your own mistrust. You've let that have more than enough power for way too long a time. This is your chance, Sam. Your chance to see what really is worth seeing. Roland said it was up to you, don't forget. Don't let the fear get to you. Remember, it will bother you only as long as you let it."

For some reason this was exactly what I wanted to hear. Full steam ahead. I swallowed and shut my mouth. I wanted to hear more.

"This is how it works Sam," he continued slowly. "That little piece of paper that Roland gave you is your ticket to the outside. There's gonna be an advisor waiting for you when you reach the end of the tunnel. Her name is Stella. She's a great gal..." He paused here, laughed slightly, then continued, "you'll know what

I'm talking about when you see her. She'll help you with what comes next. That's all that's needed to be said, Sam. You just get to Stella, hold on to your box, and everything else will take care of itself."

"You're not gonna tell me about the tunnel?" I asked.

There was a short silence.

"Nothing to tell. Just keep your eye out for Stella and keep moving forward." He patted me on the upper part of my back. I could perceive that he wanted to get away from solemnity for the time being. He tried really hard to make me feel comfortable. I will never forget him. "You just keep your eye on the prize my friend," he said in a hushed manner, "and you will be amazed like you never been amazed. This is only the beginning."

Chuck basically relayed everything I would need to know about the tunnel without actually saying anything about it. It was something that had to be done, but apparently not without reason. It was part of the deal. Just pick up and go. Full Steam Ahead. He had already been on the outside. He had seen it. Lived it. But he was stationed here now. Why? I don't know. Maybe that's just how it went... maybe you rotate in cycles... Maybe it was too much to take out there? Maybe he was needed here, that in his nature, his value was unparalleled. That sounded about right to me. I don't know. But these were questions that didn't seem to belong in this climate, in this realm, in this world where mystery was the common denominator. The penetrating curiosity to open my box superceded any fear I had about entering the tunnel. But the fear was definitely there, and I understood all too soon why Chuck refrained from going into any detail the first moment I walked through.

◆

The thing I remembered most was the cold. It started in the marrow of my bones and pervaded my entire body, like being slowly ushered into a meat locker. Everything was dark, yet not entirely. It was akin to the type of light that hit the Earth when a sinking half moon showered its rays over everything, leaving traces and outlines of terrain, too opaque for acute details, yet not unwavering to the point of dull blackness. It obtained an opalescent and translucent effect whereby the traveler was permitted to endure the twilight that seemed engraved in the walls and tubular channel that laid ahead. The air was dry yet chilled. It was like breathing tiny glass particles I remember, that scathed the inner lining of your esophagus. The ground was wet, and it appeared the entire tunnel was flooded with about a half a foot of water. And the moaning was unbearable! Faint, distant moans bellowed throughout the passage. Whence they came from, I hadn't a clue. They started and stopped with an eerie, precise repetition. When they started it was as if they emanated from the inside of your head, leaving you breathless and frozen. When they ceased, the silence that followed was so ominous, that you could barely convince your feet to start stepping. As a matter of fact the entire journey took placed on tip toe, if I remember correctly. Shivering, stammering, shaking, scrupulous toes that ever treaded that hollow. The sounds were not necessarily the moans of agony or pain, but of a somewhat pragmatic nature, as though the moaner was announcing that he or she was still present, that the very moan itself was an affirmation of existence.

The crescent walls seemed to be alive. Movement was the embodiment of this cavernous hole. Everything was motion, to the point where I got the impression that the very tunnel itself was a living entity. Such a feeling of dread that blasted my constitution. This was the nightmare that refused to allay. A thin film of sweat lied between my hardened palm and the hallowed box I was carrying. I now

clutched it like it was a sacred child, pressed against

my chest, with both hands firmly gripped. I had the

terrifying vision that it would slip out of my hands

and be lost on the eternal puddle below, float away to

some nearby embankment forever encased in

darkness, and that eventually, I too, would become a

fixture in the permanent night of this journey, etched

as a perverse addition to the gallery of moaners.

I looked ahead and behind me rapidly, ever so

often, while trudging onward. I could see nothing

behind me. What little I could see before me was

nothing short of misery, for the very fact that there

laid a promise in the view, that never bridged any

progress or form of gradual proximity. There

appeared to be an opening ahead. Shafts of thinly

framed light burst then dimmed in the distance, outlining what seemed to be a semblance of an exit. The problem was that I never gained any ground. The more I advanced the less it seemed I traversed any territory, the exit never nearing, the light further away. This put me in such a state of exhaustion and confusion that I sat on a large rock in the pathway, breathing unevenly, spinning with thoughts that assailed me from every direction.

I was stupefied that only a moment ago, I was feeling peaceful, at ease, that I was on a collision course with destiny, that everything seemed orderly, fit to perfection, purposeful; that just moments prior I was talking with Chuck, and now I am here, where night had steeled my inner world. I even forgot what Chuck looked like. I couldn't picture him at all. I suddenly had the unnerving thought that everything I experienced before was nothing but a dream, a wild hallucination. I felt a planetary fatigue oppress my limbs and I stretched out on the boulder as much as I could, bringing my knees up slightly, lying perpendicular, almost in a fetal position. I used the white leather box as a cushion under my head. I wanted now more than ever to open the box, and finally see what all the mystery was. The moaning ceased temporarily. A dialogue ensued.

I told myself that this could be the last chance to do anything, that my death could be imminent, and remembered Roland's commandment to open it in private. There were no spectators I could see anywhere. I even began questioning the importance of this white rectangle and wondered If I had been duped, and made a fool. How could I fall for all this magical, mystical, spooky-hooey? I felt a fury rising up in me producing a resurgence that demanded I open the box. The impatient, surly, mathematical side of me was winning the argument. Reason and logic, which seemed absent throughout this free fall, now towered above all, taking full command of my faculties. I raised my head, stood up, and looked around. Nothing, nobody. I hesitated, took a deep breath, then moved to open the lid. My hand trembled, wet with perspiration. The dam thing wouldn't open. The lid seemed frozen shut. At first I pried gently, but to no avail, then firmer: nothing. My anger, frustration, coldness, and fear reached such a culminating apex that I turned beastly, and stomped on the box ravenously, cursing the thing, feeling like an utter fool, confirmed in all my suspicions that I would die muted, unknown, in this terrible tunnel. I picked up the container, resolute to fling it far into the recesses.

"I wouldn't do that, If I were you," a voice spoke behind me.

I turned around frantically. A woman stood before me. She had curly, blonde hair, emerald eyes, with youthful, luminous skin. She looked to be in her early twenties, wearing a pea-green, cloth dress that fit tightly around her plump figure. Her expression bore a solemn shade yet cordial, and I sensed impatience residing in the movement of her shoulders.

"Who are you?" I asked, slightly pained by the dryness of my throat, spellbound with curiosity.

She anticipated this and dipped a clay bowl in the water below and handed it to me.

"It's okay, drink it," she said, responding to my reluctance to accept the bowl.

I drank like lightning, coughing and heaving at first, then slowly drank some more. It was the best water I ever tasted. I felt immediately refreshed. She took my hand. We walked together side by side. I noticed her feet were bare, and glistened with tiny droplets dispersing on each foot as they rose out of what became a tiny stream below us. Every time she looked at me in the eyes I felt a new wave of conviction and strength to keep moving, stay afloat. The cold didn't bother me as much now.

"Here's the thing Sam," she slowly began, "Oh,

don't forget that," she said, indicating the leather box. I went back and quickly thrust it into my arms.

"I really shouldn't have stopped you. Actually it's against the rules," she said.

She took a deep breath. "But I had no idea how long you were gonna be, and I got things to do." She apprehended that I was teetering on disbelief and total collapse, so she didn't hold anything back. "You see, you were supposed to come to befriend the tunnel, and learn to accept the path in the presence of fear, transcending your other self, thereby enhancing you to the next level, and allowing you admittance to the outside. That's the whole point of the tunnel. It's not something random and capricious, a little something we like to torture you with, not at all. It's invented by you, you created all of this."

"But why? What for?" I asked, almost breathlessly.

"Oh boy, here we go. Chuck warned me about you," she said, with a gentle smile, not in the least bit admonishing.

"Is Chuck here?"

"It's important that you heed what I say" she said, and we stopped walking.

"What's your name by the way?" I inquired.

"Not important, just listen," she said exhaling big, "I really gotta get a new gig," she said, rubbing her forehead. "You have to understand that this is not a process that is easily explained. There are really good reasons why you don't understand certain things. That's what we don't get the first run around. It's a privilege to not know, not a burden. But, for your sake I can tell you that it all has something to do with the way you came here."

"You're Stella!" I said.

"That's right, putting it all together now, are we?"

"Chuck told me about you."

"That's great, but do you mind if we continue this outside?"

"We're going outside?" I said, with a failed attempt at suppressing exhilaration, which came flooding into my chest.

"Not unless you wanna stick around here," she said, with a smile that sent me reeling.

I had this overwhelming urge to plant a huge kiss on her vermouth lips. It took everything I had to bury this yearning. I think she sensed this, and turned away from me quickly. We resumed walking. The light became bigger as we advanced, until it shrouded us completely, enveloping everything. I thought I saw a tree in the distance with a bird lighting on its branch. The colors were unspeakable.

◆

"Absolutely amazing," I cried.

"Yes, it is."

Open expanses of grass and wheat spread out far and wide. The back drop was an ocean the color of smooth glass, not a breath of wind stirred. Big, robust trees stood towering and picturesque in sparse numbers far apart from each other, claiming their own plot of land. The sky conveyed a nearing sunset light that bathed the land in gold and amber, but obtained a lavender, rose, and slightly pink tone that swirled up above. There was no sun in sight, and I noticed none of the trees or more elevated terrain cast any shadows upon the ground. The sounds of waves breaking, birds chirping, and the cawing of crows, filled the air and resonated an awe-inspiring soundtrack to the unspeakable colors and landscape that fit together, in my mind, in complete harmony.

"You got something for me?" Stella asked,

breaking my spell.

"What?"

"That little note that Roland gave you back at the office? I need it."

"Oh, that," I said, ransacking my pockets, fumbling and stammering. I flushed it out and handed it to her. "What does it say, anyway?"

You didn't read it?" She asked, surprised somewhat.

"It didn't even occur to me."

"It's just something for the records, no need to worry about it."

She rolled up the little note and stuck it in her tuft of curls, as though it was a detailed filing system for her, and whenever she wanted to retrieve it again, she could do so blindly.

After a moment I asked, "This must be heaven. Right?"

She pointed at the white leather box that was tucked under my left arm. "Just follow the song of the crow."

"Song of the crow?"

She gestured with her eyes behind me, toward the west. I turned to look. There, in plain view was a large Elm tree adorned with a flock of crows cawing, singing, flying momentarily then alighting back on the Elm's supple branches. I turned back around and met her V-shaped back, walking away from me. She was a good ten yards away and I wanted to call out to her, but inclined not to. I would have never made it out of that tunnel without Stella's intervention, one that she openly admitted was a break in the rules, and when I saw her walking away from me I instantly knew that she didn't have anything pressing to do and that I would see her again, and that if I didn't have that assurance, none of this– the sky, the ocean, the fields, the peace, and the white leather box– would have meant anything. How I knew this I knew not, but I was tired of asking questions. All at once the disquiet of my mind hushed. I was struck with an immense calm.

I strolled to the Elm with the nonchalant walk of a man who finally realized what it meant to be able to walk on his own two feet. I savored every footstep, every breath, every image my eyes rested on. I sat down at the base of the tree, the box laid flat on my lap. I slowly opened the lid with great ease, and inside was a single, 8 x 10, black and white photograph of my grandmother in her prime, looking at me with elegant grace underneath a faint smile. I felt warm all over. I raised my head and standing before me was Stella, smiling the smilingest smile, her hand stretched out to me. Behind her, sitting in row upon row, slowly ascending the distant hills, all facing me, was everyone.

Dr. Kelly Buffone

The Indelible Stamina of Mason Muslevitch

After everything had been depleted. After all the nagging reminders of what lay ahead were absorbed by the whirlwind of the last woman. There it was again. The unremitting pursuit of total annihilation. Upon me in yet another package of chocolate curves and fleshy brilliance. In life you never get what you want. Never. You believe you've attained something that was held in high regard by all your faculties and

loins respectfully and you are bitterly crushed by the

waning desire that burns out. Slowly and gradually.

To the point where you fight with yourself. Pulling out

your hair. Disgusted. As to why you wanted her in the

first place. Everything should stay in your

imagination. Keep it locked there forever. Guard it

against any form of fruition.

I kept dreaming about dried leaves. Standing on

the deck of some ship. Not exactly sunny. But no sign

of rain. A thin mist hovered over everything. Not a

normal mist. A mist that can only be found in dreams.

Thousands of dried leaves. Strewn all over the vessel.

I adopted the usual attitude. The absence of all

disbelief. Like gullible rain drops. The casual

demeanor that all this is entirely normal. Perfect

sense. Sailing. Dead leaves. I always wake up when I see a figure behind the wheel. Again no surprise. I can never make out a concrete acknowledgment of who or what is doing the steering. A faceless morph. Air and shadow. Breathless and heaving. I always feel like it is me. Something always tells me. Something winks. Something always winks. Instincts that can only reside in dreams. The figure has the same shoulders as I do. Like an indescribable truth. The intangible understanding. That we are breathing. The figure lends a familiarity.

The moment a dream is diverted from its current saga and the scene is about to change, which happens very often with me, with absolutely no relevance to the subsequent scenario, I am never flummoxed. I ease into the changes. Without the slightest feeling of agitation. I simply move on. Like a Hindu cow. Grazing the next patch of earth. Content with my insignificance. Immersed in spiritual repose. It's only in life where the chaos is terrifying. Undone. Battered. A bloody pulp of mashed nerves. I should have let her stay in my head. It's much safer there.

"Was that just a one time deal?" the text message read. Text messaging is the battle of glaciers. The deadliest form of communication. All the emotions: The stifling awkwardness. The clumsy search for dignified responses. Personal accountability. All removed. Language dangling. Standing alone in digital revelry. Cold. It allots you time to think of more clever ways to lie. Another invention that decreases the humanity in all of us. Yay for technology. You win again. Maybe the movies were actually hitting on something. We will all become compliant to machines. Mechanization. Dependent. Any significant breakdown in the system will lead to our demise. I don't think it's that fantastical a thought. You think that if John Adams and Jefferson texted each other back and forth that anything would have been accomplished?

I stared at the screen of the cell phone. Her words dripped in pleading. Like a sad pair of corduroy pants. Yearning for clarity. I could picture her going to sleep every night with one last thought poking her: He didn't call again. Wtf? I hated to make her feel that way. It certainly wasn't fair. I was cognizant of the crushing fact that there was enough unfairness in one's life that my adding to that pile was beyond degrading. I sent her a couple of texts supporting her innocence and my depravity. Feeble attempts to place all the blame on myself. Then she sent me a message that broke my heart in two.

"I feel kinda sad. Is that silly? You're a great guy. Good luck."

What is it that resides in all of us which desires decadence? Unflinching vulgarity. Animalistics. Carnivorous consumption. Good old fashioned barbarism. At the same time is woeful. Empathetic. Tender. Horrifically sentimental. And easily bowled over? No matter what we come up with there will never be a creation as complex as a human being. I hope I get a chance to meet that twisted artist.. Boy do I have some cross examining to purge.

"Are all the handbags fifty percent off?" an older

lady asked me from the back of the store. Diverting my attention. Squawky voice. Wearing a lime-colored garment of some sorts. She looked like an ostrich dipped in kiwi juice. I nodded my head wearily. It was the day of the big sale. The women were ruthlessly carousing the aisles. Dipping their hands in every purse. Slipping their feet into all the sandals with Roman delight. Hungry like the moon. Starved for commerce. I sat there behind the register. Celine's first book on the counter. Cowering. Trying to remember why I gave out favors. Someone once said a favor will kill you faster than a bullet. Wasn't halfway untrue. A conversation between two ladies that looked to be in their early forties within ear shot.

Lady #1: I think I know what Sally's problem is.

Lady # 2: Oh yeah?

Lady # 1: She is too negative. I told her that the reason she is unhappy is that she is just too negative.

Lady # 2: That's a good point. I always thought that.

Lady # 1: She is so immature sometimes. I tried to tell her about my positive reinforcement plan, you know the one I learned at the seminar, and she scoffed.

Lady #2: What is she taking?

Lady #1: Nothing.

Lady #2: Nothing?

Lady #1: Can you believe it?

Lady #2: Unreal. I am taking Parantol for anxiety, Caratol for depression, and Boost 300 for my fatigue. I can't live without them.

Lady #1: I explained to her that there are many ways to combat her disorder, but she doesn't seem interested in any form of self evaluation.

Lady #2: Doesn't she realize she needs help? She must be in heavy denial.

At this point Lady #1 looks over at me with a trendy yellowish summer bag. "How much is this?"

"There should be a price tag on the handle," I said.

"Do you have this in red?"

"I really don't know. I'm am just watching the store for a friend. But she told me that everything is on the floor, so if we do, it should be around." I could tell that my remarks annoyed her slightly. She was an aristocrat of the proudest order. Used to everyone beckoning to her. Toppling mountains to supplicate her. I felt a strong sensation that if we were living in Elizabethan times I would have been beheaded for such inadequateness. Their conversation veered back in forth between their friend's negativeness and their children's track record for disobedience. The nagging. Unrelenting nagging. That is what it all comes to when dreams are demolished. You become a nag box. There is nothing left for you to aspire for. Nothing to accomplish. The heartbreak that stings you in late youth ferments into concrete bitterness as the wrinkles and grey hairs appear. Out of nowhere. In the middle of the night. Popping up fresh and anew.

You look into that god awful mirror unprepared to face a new day. I always liked the term looking glass. All the modern terms lack soul for that matter. But I don't mean to digress...

The nagging faded as the women left the shop. Silence returned. The temperature got slightly cooler as the sun made its descent. Everything took on a lonely tint. The flower sandals shrieked. The store moaned. The air wept. The parking lot was near empty. I eyed the text message once again. I wanted to tell her more but felt so little and helpless. I thought of my mother. I went outside. Cigarette Fix. I noticed three youngsters carrying skateboards entering the plaza. One of them stared. A dirty blonde haired boy. Loose clothing. A day of adventure on his face. Gentle eyes. Soft gait. A note of mischief played in his movements. His look could disintegrate kingdoms.

Immediately I became frantic. Cautious. A stumbling

mess of nervosity. He is still looking. Why? What for?

He moves to speak.

"Hey, how are you? Having a nice day?" the boy

said to me, coming to a full stop.

"I'm fine," I stammered, eying the back of his

two friends as they continued through the plaza.

"What are you doing? Just hanging around?"

"I'm working," I said, a bit calmed by the tone of

his voice, but brimming with confusion, and hoping he

would move on.

"Where? In the handbag shop?" The boy said.

Real nice like. Not a glimmer of malice in his

intonations. "You don't look like a handbag guy, that's

for sure." He laughed a small laugh. Electricity exuded from his vibrant face. I squirmed.

"I'm watching it for a friend."

"Okay, well, I gotta get going now. Have a wonderful evening."

The boy smiled big and bright. Turned around. Walked off. What the hell was that? Suspicions flared inside my mind. Turning. Bending. Twisting around that uncharacteristically sweet soul. I looked up. Behind me. Around me. Then back in the store. A thought emblazoned. Maybe some sort of conspiracy was taking place? Maybe the boy was a diversion? Maybe cohorts were inside the store ransacking everything? Rapid mind crunch. Twirling cerebellum inferno. I inspected the handbags. Cash register.

Found nothing out of the ordinary. I slumped down in my chair. The cover of Celine's novel staring at me. I went back outside. I watched the people walking down Main Street. I wondered to myself suddenly if I would have been so skeptical of any outright display of benevolence five or maybe even two years ago. I found myself utterly dejected with the way I processed things nowadays. Cynicism. The ultimate death of any living thing. Streamed its way into my veins. An obstacle to self. When I think of the word cynical I always defer to the Oscar Wilde definition: 'A cynic is someone who knows the price of everything but the value of nothing.'

With every waking minute of consciousness the murdering continues. The complete desecration of perceiving the essence of things. A trait that blossoms with birth and deteriorates with time. Envelopes your days and nights. I thought of Salinger and how dead on he was. Was I finally falling over that precipice? Taking the big plunge? Have I reached the last refrain of an idyllic youth? If so, why was I not scratching? Fighting? Clinging with every fiber of my being to hold onto the last shreds of it? Why am I so aloof? Maybe this is what happens to everyone. To my father even. One day the fighter in you just packs it in and hangs his gloves. Refusing to endure another heart wrenching blow. Comfort and solace become the only modes of existence. The main priorities. And we all know that whatever spectacular magic that ever emanated from this sad-blue earth never arose out of meager safety.

My phone rang. It was Brody.

"Hey Mason, whatcha doing?"

"Nothing special. Watching the store for Denise."

"That sucks. When are you off?"

I looked at the credit card screen. It read seven thirty. "Probably in a half," I said.

"Wanna meet at church?" Brody said. "I really had a shitty day, and I ain't got nothing else to do. Unless of course you're meeting that girl..."

"Nah, I'll meet you there."

"Cool. First round on me."

Brody was a gambler. Itchy. Twitchy. Mad rush seeker. He once lost a bet and had to go watch 'Schindler's List' (when it was released theatrically), and laugh hysterically whenever someone died. You can imagine what happened to him. I believe he still has problems hearing out of his left ear.

I hung up the phone. Twilight showered everything. The parking lot was full of oil stains. I got up. Turned out the lights. Locked up the store. And headed out with the brain scorching awareness that another misstep laid in the crevices.

◆

We drank heavily. The night hooted and hollered for it. Our lonesomeness bleeded profusely. Everybody looked the part. Brains inside thick domes.

Eyes curled up next to that smoky woman hissing back at everything you fire. Sipping that coolness of hops and grains. God kissing your lips. We get bludgeoned for our innocence. It makes you wonder. What if the devil isn't a bad fella after all? What if there's boredom in heaven? What if its downright unbearable? I always saw outlaws before heroes. Scowls before smiles. I never trusted a smile. I smiled a lot these days. It was the best form of deception. We drank radically. We were tired of being afraid. Afraid of Everything. Our fathers never told us the truth. I resented him. Until later. We can never accept our father until later. The truth can never be told. Otis Redding howling every bit of sadness that resided in the molecules of our empty cups. Fill her up Bobby. Bobby was young. He was clueless. He looked the part. Eyes still vibrant. Ignorant Vigor. Dumb organism of youth. Hope was often alluded to in his private underwear dreams. As it should be. With glistening shoulders his thoughts cemented on lily breasts. Lilac flavored vaginas. Preoccupation with mandom. His armpits were blossoming. The young have their priorities. Coming and leaving. Sensory orgiastic enterprise. They'll kill their brothers for just a droplet. The elixir of transparent blouses. The drinking was voracious. I could read his thoughts on the gang of us. What a bunch of pathetic losers. He wasn't wrong. I could hear his conversations with his girlfriend after the foxes went to sleep.

How was work sweety? Work sucked. Why? I am sick and tired of serving pathetic losers. I want more. Oh don't worry baby. You will get all you want. I know. If I ever turn out like the guys that come to my bar, shoot me. You won't. I love you. I love you too. Smooches and slurps. Gropes and grinds. Legs and fingertips. Necks and sweats. Fondling aflame. Zygote Power. The world grows. The Earth rejoices. Toddler fever rises to their brows.

The sun must be sickened at what it sees. I empathize with the sun. I apologize to the sun. Is there anything lonelier than the sun? Is there a worker more dedicated to duty than the sun? And we worship men... Fill her up Bobby.

The morning came sloppily. Stillness. Silence. The only hint of life was the trembling of leaves on the maple that crowded my window. It was too quiet. I couldn't hear my breathing. I felt that the world had been unplugged. Unspeakable fear rising. This is it.

Again no resistance. Aloof. Unchained to anything on this plane. I was ready like Freddy. My eyes closed. The dream that keeps dreaming. Leaves. Boats. Shadows.

I entered the office. He sat pondering something more important. He didn't notice me for awhile. I sat down in the chair opposite. A coffee table separated us. Deepak Chopra's eternally smiling face staring me down. He was too clean for me. He looked like a penny that had never seen a hand in its life. Hair perfect. Teeth whiter than his masters. De-human. I wanted to tell him that if he wore a shirt with a ripped pocket people like me would listen more. Oh, and stop smiling for chrissakes. I don't think a tire iron to the head could remove that plastered smile. But he didn't need people like me. He counted on people like me to dismiss him. And we did. He had plenty of corvette dads and bridal shower moms to lean on. There was a lot of confusion out there. His market was endless.

A photograph of a little girl in blond pig tails sat on a desk behind the shrink. By the way he still didn't notice me at this point. I am pretty forgetful and un-memorable. But now I feel invisible. I couldn't help but feel sorry for that little girl in the photo. I wanted to kiss her cheeks and lay my hand across her eyes forever. Live blind little one. Avert your eyes at all costs. Emotions swelled. Pity rose. I wanted to father that child and work on an interplanetary project of magnificent proportions. I wanted to build that little one a private refuge on Neptune. A ladder to the furthest constellation. With all that universe you would think a father - a caring and concerned one -

would find a place that could accommodate. A new

beginning. Polluteless matter. Atmospheric regalia.

New fruit to chomp on. A new diamond sky.

I once knew a father whose child fell to cancer.

He said something to me I will never forget. 'The thing

that broke my heart more than his death was the look

he gave me while he was dying. He looked at me with

broken faith. His father, who was always there to help

him with anything, couldn't move Heaven and Earth

to save him. A father must always be able to move

Heaven and Earth.' I tried to tell him that most fathers

were assholes. He agreed. Mentioned that him and his

father would end in fisticuffs all the time when he was

a youth. But he believed in an ideal. He stood for

something beyond himself. Beyond reason. Beyond

possibility. I wondered if I ever believed in anything

like that.

Her name is Jasmine. The doctor shook from his thought dreams. He had the soul of a paper lantern. I was the village square. Where all the muddy footsteps trudged. I received phlegm well. He received tans well. His walls were covered with photos of himself sandwiched between old white men. Ghosts. Faceless. Nameless. Hairless. Golfers.

You can't go on like this Mason. He wasn't entirely wrong. He had the voice of a studied assassin. Hushed Terror. Creases on his face convulsed. I didn't want to go on like this. One never wants to go on like this. Every textbook he ever read came out of his mouth. I was still invisible. He played with his chin. He was a chin rubber. I wondered how his chin felt about that. Was it mutual or was he raping his chin at will?

We ended with him brightening a smile like an infomercial host. He wanted to put me on drugs. I didn't want any of their drugs. I wanted my own drugs. I was afraid their drugs might turn me into them. I would rather go mad. Hair ripping psycho. Bona fide mess. Meltdown for the ages. Fill her up Bobby.

Bobby talked obediently. He wasn't interested. I could hear his manager's coaching. Always smile. Make small talk. Never too personal. Enthusiasm is infectious. Make the customer feel like furniture. At all costs. Silence = no tips. I tried to be polite. Obliging. People don't come to a bar to make friends. They come to escape them. Greet their enemies. Slap darkness on the back. Mingle with themselves. Destroy the black smudges smeared on them. Repent.

Sanctify. Cleanse. Throw their souls in a washer. Pour the Vodka. Turn the dial. Rinse. Dry. A brand new canvass. Hopeful. We are all hopeful. Hopeful that the portrait will look different. It never does. It only becomes harder to see ourselves.

In she walked. Prowess. Curled lips. Dipped hips. Glossy toes with Chopin's nose. The enemy of all enemies. I was unguarded. Unfounded. Faltering. Fortressless. I felt a surge. Like an electrocuted minnow. Lazered loins. This is how wars are started. Something winks. War. Please god. Say it ain't so. She uncoiled. Bobby filled her up.

NO GPS

It started out terribly sour, the two of us together for a whole three days. Anybody with me for longer than twenty four hours could tell you that I become unbearably gloomy and moody, a trait I have never been able to avoid, something that must have been passed down to me from a long line of dejected grumpsters. Something always comes over me, like a dark cloud looming in the distance, which eventually becomes legible in my face, a scowl for the ages, which is why solitude has always been my most faithful companion. We didn't say a word to each other as we packed our small luggage sacks into the trunk. Her mother stood by the doorway, with a look on her face that knew me better than I wanted her to. She was poised and well trained at her age. She showed no outward signs that she was irritated by me seeing her daughter. But the glimmer in her eyes spoke volumes, and she hugged me mechanically, cautiously, like a hit man who doesn't want to alert his prey to any oncoming slaughter.

"Do you have any books in the car," I ask her as we drive away from the house.

"Yeah, I have a couple in the trunk," she says as she turns on the stereo.

"Never mind."

"I have Ulysses in the back seat," she says as she reached toward the back seat. She laid the great Irish novel in my lap. It was a new edition with some sort of modern, pizzazz design on the cover. It was heavier than I remembered it to be.

"Have you ever read it before?"

"I tried to a long time ago," I mumbled. "But I never got around to finishing it."

"It's really good, one of my favorite books."

I immediately felt this disgust for the book. I flipped to the introduction quickly. The editor started kissing Joyce's ass right off the bat. Introductions always annoyed me. But remember I was already annoyed. By what? God knows. For some reason I was always one that shied away from any semblance of contentment that life might have presented me. I felt most alive when struggling, displaced, striving forward, fleeing, from what and why, who the hell knew? And I guess, now that I look back at that, I can't really say "alive" but rather, less dead.

She twisted the volume knob on the stereo blaring out the latest top ten hits she compiled on a CD. We used to call them mix tapes, but I think they are something entirely different now. The music made me restless, stabbed at my ears. It all sounded so defective to me. The lyrics were trite and filled with a particular type of arrogance that made me feel tremulous, shifty in my seat, almost like I was suffocating. I buried my face in the book. I gave her a sidelong glance. She was bouncing in her seat, weaving through traffic, carefree, and jubilant, singing along with the tunes, oblivious to anything. I winced on the inside. I told myself to just ignore it, don't let it bother you, but we all know how futile those requests to ourselves are. I wondered how anybody could be that inconsiderate, that impervious to someone sitting right next to you, someone who was obviously not amused, practically rubbing shoulders with you. I mean, I understand it's her car, and she invited me on this trip, but I payed for the gas, bought other miscellaneous things. I'm a passenger, a supposed guest that she so eagerly wanted to have along with her, a human being with a heart and soul, and does she really have to listen to it that LOUD?? The speakers reverberated, the windows shook with every electronic drum beat. How can anyone enjoy this?

"Oh shit, I knew this would happen."

I looked up from the book and realized what she was talking about. The freeway was jammed with cars, traffic came to a stifling five miles an hour. Great, I said to myself, now I have to listen to this shit she is playing for even longer.

"Do you think you could turn it down just a little?" I asked. She lowered the volume silently, without even looking over at me. "You don't have to if that's how you like it ..."

"It's fine," she spoke sternly.

I went back to the book. Tension seized the interior of that automobile and squeezed the life out of everything, especially me. We strolled down the road on that hot summer day in silence for an hour. I tried to read the adventure of Dedalus but found myself utterly distracted, discombobulated, unnerved. I kept re-reading the same passages over and over again, causing my head to throb. We exited on to an off ramp, silent as ever. We had gone two hours with no conversation. A woman who can hold their tongue for that long is pretty impressive, I remembered thinking at the time. Even if they are driven by ignorance rather than spite, for silence is much harder to achieve when fueled by spite, it takes a true professional to carry that off; the fact that she held her ground and didn't give in to anything rummaging inside her, for there was no doubt she was ruminating over things, caught me off guard. You can tell when people have images, memories, and other vague scenarios swimming in their head by the way their neck and shoulders move, by the way their lips mumble wordlessly. There is a look in their eyes that is seeing everything and nothing at the same time. I looked at her a little differently after that.

"Are you hungry?" she asked.

"Are you?"

"Yeah, but I want coffee first."

"What are our options?"

"Fast food," she said.

She looked at me as she said that and for the

first time, in what seemed to be forever, I was able to see what she held in those two almond orbs. Nothing. Absolutely nothing, as if she was talking to a postman, accepting a delivery, signing for a package, her eyes revealed none of the turmoil that I was feeling. And for some sick, demented reason that infuriated me. Is she just a really good actress? Or is she that completely heartless? I began to feel heavy in my chest, blood was boiling, and a few beads of sweat formed on my forehead.

"Okay, well... um...I dunno about fast food, I kinda wanted something different."

"This is the only stop for food for the next forty five miles," she said.

"What do you want?"

"Wendy's."

"Okay."

"There's a subway on the other side of the freeway, we could go there," she said.

I didn't feel like eating anymore.

"It doesn't matter."

"Are you sure?"

"Yeah."

She drove to the coffee drive thru. I looked out the window to the expansive plains. The sun was low. A blanket of blue was dressing the Earth. The kind of blue that can only be found in a California twilight. Subtle, swallowing, soothing, the air became slightly cooler, prospects were more ominous, faces appeared more solemn. The Earth never fell asleep soundly. There is always something lurking in that transitional silence when the night tip toes into the sky, something hideous, fretful, and revealing. The mask was coming off. We no longer needed gloves. We no longer needed to talk. The night let us know where we stood. We understood each other better than we ever did as she ordered her vanilla latte. I felt relieved. I looked at her as she took a tentative sip of the hot drink. She noticed me looking at her.

"What?" she said with a confused smile.

"Nothing."

"Wendy's?"

"Absolutely," I said.

Harry's Request

Harry felt like a fraud, like someone who had spent the last thirty-five years of his life fooling himself and his family into thinking he had a true talent, that he was gifted in a way that separated him from the rest of the hungry men that occupied the world of piano players. He sat on the veranda of the home he had built with his father when he was just a child. He was his father's age now, at the time he died, and he could still see the cracks in the wooden railing that they would argue over time and time again, like all fathers and sons do, when trying to be men in front of one another. A father always has an inherent need to outshine his son, no matter how much pride and love he bestows upon him. It goes back to the animal kingdom; a primordial trait ingrained in the male species, and about as refutable as gravity. No matter how humble or harmless a man seems, there is a part of him that will always seek recognition and approbation from his peers and kin alike, and sometimes that man will manifest very "primitive," if not downright barbaric advancements for his cause. Without it a man is a gnat, a nothing, a splotch of phlegm on a weathered sidewalk. Harry thought of this as he sat quietly on his favorite chair, minutes away from twilight. His sixty third birthday was coming the next day and his wife had prepared a bash of sorts, inviting family, and friends, and even a few neighbors that were agreeable. He wasn't looking forward to it. He wanted nothing more than a simple evening of dinner, his favorite cigar, a snifter of brandy, and time alone to sit out in the open air with god and his memories as his only faithful companions.

Night after night he would look forward to that time of evening, just as the sun was setting over the California horizon, a horizon, unlike any other in the world, where the dance between light, color, water, and sky was violently magnified; a sort of slaughter of the day, rather than a dying, as they say. The horizon was etched in purple, violet, and amber, and seemed to go on forever into the outer depths of the sky. A cosmic war that took place every day at dusk, leaving a bloodstained battlefield for all the coast to witness. It always put Harry in the perfect, contemplative mood, setting his thoughts aflame, as the repose of the neighborhood and everything in it gave his dreaming no deterrence, allowed his memories to sail freely to him, one after another, some more inviting than others, and then a few he would have liked to incinerate, never to appear before his eyes again.

He started playing piano later in life, around his teenage years, which was traditionally too late, in the realm of musicianship, first starting with rock and roll. The high booming wail of Little Richard and his maniacal pounding of the ivory keys was all that consumed Harry in the beginning. He never liked the virtuosity of Jazz, and all of its elemental components,

too much in too little a measure, he always thought.

Not enough room to breathe, to allow the melody to

evolve, with most of the attention focused on

mechanics, for Jazz, he always said, was a true

craftsman's vocation. A jester could never sit on the

throne of a King, is how he paralleled the relationship

between jazz and rock music. A rock musician payed

no mind to how polished they played, or how "off" the

music seemed, theoretically. Theory was thrown out

the window, almost mocked in a way, math was

replaced by raw emotion, and lyrics were sprinkled

on top, as the aesthetic forerunner. They were knights

jousting it out across the American musical landscape,

and Rock was winning in Harry's mind. The

irreverence of rock and roll appealed to him the most,

and he was a natural. And he knew there wasn't a book in the world, or a course you could take, or a seminar, that could teach one to spill that much soul onto a stage as Little Richard did. So, he played and pounded, and created a racket, much to the dismay of his Father, doing everything he could to emulate what he heard those rock pioneers doing on records.

Harry lit his cigar as the plaintive melody of the crickets and buzzing, flying critters consumed the air, and he thought about how boundless his dreams were back then. He remembered that he had visions of touring with Little Richard and Chuck Berry, sitting in on piano, just a part of the scene, for he couldn't sing, and his writing abilities extended to signing his name and placing the date on a piece of paper, and even

that, was imbued with errors. He knew all the popular
rock songs of his day note for note, measure to
measure. He remembered the insidious air of
confidence he would exude every day in school,
knowing somehow, that his dreams were not just
something to help him sleep at night, but were cold
hard facts, and there was no reason he could think of,
in his adolescent naivete, that could impede him from
achieving them. "Oh, the folly of youth," Harry could
hear his father tell him with a giant sigh.

He thought of his father a lot lately. He didn't
know why and he was somewhat irked that the image
of him wouldn't leave him alone, especially during the
times he wanted the night to himself, alone,
underneath the celestial sky, with clouds of tobacco

smoke and cheap brandy he would sip slowly with a sense of ceremony and relish, as if it were imported. The lingering oils from the leaves of smoke mingled exuberantly with the viscous, double distilled spirit as he pressed his tongue firmly against the roof of his mouth after each swallow.

His father was the "inaccessible" type, someone who didn't show his emotions, and reserved praise for people outside of his family, which always pained Harry to observe, but, much like his father, would never let on how much it distressed him. Conversations were about as fluid as playing soccer on an active volcano; trouble festering in every crevice of the exchange, a hint of chastisement coated on every word, a throttling lying in the mist, like a patient panther waiting in the bush for its prey. Harry remembered how he would go to great lengths to try and avoid any situation where they would be forced to talk, or where a chat might have room to develop. He reflected, slightly sadly, how when Saturday mornings arrived he would lock himself in his room, without ever leaving it, waiting anxiously by the door, listening for those infamous boot sounds smacking the hard floor that would indicate his dad leaving the house for the racetrack, something he would always do on Saturday. Once those Macy's brand, pseudo cowboy boots started rapping on the pavement, an immense relief filled him, and the tension in his back and neck would subside, almost like a fawn realizing that imminent peril has receded, that the hunter had been evaded, and tranquility was upon the land again.

Once in a while his father would skip the track, and those were the days of sheer anguish, when Harry felt like a prisoner, shackled to his bedroom, like an Arabian thief. "Those boots," Harry said to himself with a wry smile, shaking his head slowly. If ever there was an article of clothing that could encapsulate a person, those boots, Harry thought, were the very personification of father.

When Harry discovered Chopin, everything changed for him. The ideas of musical progression, dynamism, subtlety, and nuance were elevated to an all time high and his obsession took on profound proportions. Rock and Roll became a casual hobby. He studied and sweat classical forms, digested everything Chopin published, and became a mildly accomplished pianist, but his dream was to compose, and to become a legendary composer. Harry was assailed by a memory of his father sitting in a room full of Harry's relatives and friends, all encouraging him to play for them, and allowing no excuse to justify his declining. It was a Thanksgiving party, when Harry was twenty-five, already a promising prodigy in the classical arts, attending one of the top schools for music. Harry would never forget his father's face, and how prominently it stood out from the sea of faces, as he got behind the piano. He remembered how malevolent it looked, and how dispirited he appeared, *his father* while everyone else, including his mother, and professor, beamed with pride and eagerness. Harry was dumbstruck, and immediately he felt all of his will and ability deflate and wilt, as if his father's scowl was some kind of toxin injected into his body, rendering him helpless, and numb all over. He had no command of his faculties, he was unable to conjure any reinforcements. He felt like some evil phantom had stripped him of all his talent and turned his hands into giant cinder blocks for that singular moment, like some cruel, heartless prank. It was the worst he ever played in his life. The pangs of that night's performance stung like fresh wounds that would never coagulate. Harry distinctly remembered, as if it happened not a moment ago, how the entire room was aghast, and dizziness and sweat consumed him from head to toe. He never looked up from the piano, but the immutable disappointment could be felt on the top of his head like a giant mountain landed on him. When he finished the piece, obligatory applause followed with some feigned remarks of commendation. Electric shockwaves coursed through his cheeks and he began to blink convulsively, calling all the will power he had left to come to his aid, to help him conceal his inward meltdown. He wanted to smash his head on the piano, and it took every bit of strength he had left to appear unfazed. Harry didn't come near a piano for three weeks after that night.

Harry composed a few things that received some critical acclaim, but nothing even near the vicinity of legendary status. While in his thirties and late forties he toured with some notable conductors, no one prolific, and played in a few orchestras over seas, the ghost of Chopin haunted him throughout his career, and some critics even scathed him for attempting "quite crudely" to imitate and even "plagiarize" some of Chopin's greatest works. He presently taught a composition class at his alma mater and played every now and then, more seldom than usual, in a concert performance. He recognized, with a thunderous and consummate resolve, that his dreams were exactly that, just dreams that received cultivation and nurturing in the brain of a young man, but now that brain had found a home in an old man, where fertile soil had withered and was depleted of all the nutrients needed for regeneration. They kept coming however, haunting, persistent, inexorable reveries commanded his attention. He didn't know if he wanted them to stop or not. He felt morose when he thought about the past like a fleeting dream, but he also clung to those images, savored them, relived them, heightening his sense of the tragic, the real, the

eloquent truth that was exposed to him so

incontrovertibly.

"Sweetie?" Harry's wife called from the kitchen

window directly behind him. It took her several yells

to grab Harry's attention, who was so ensconced in

his head, that when he finally turned to respond, he

was startled, and almost forgot where he was.

"Yes, what is it?"

"I wanted to ask you a question about the

party," she said raspily, and unconcernedly. "You got

two choices for food, Greek, or Chinese?"

"It doesn't really matter to me Kathy," Harry

said with some irritation that he was being reminded

of the party.

"Well, the Statler's and the Mulvey's are allergic to most of the Greek menu, so if you don't mind, I think Chinese would be adequate and less of a problem. I'm gonna get your favorite, the eggplant kung pao."

"Fine."

"Your cousin Alvin called and said he wouldn't be able to make it, but Jerry and Alice are confirmed."

"Fine."

"You gonna come in soon?" she said, while washing some dishes in the sink.

"As soon as I'm done with my cigar," Harry said trying to conceal his annoyance. Kathy walked out of the kitchen and left Harry alone. Once again, tranquility was upon the land.

The stars were popping up in the sky in faster increments, as black began its trek through the heavenly vista. It was one of those August evenings where the heat was ineffectual, and the summer wind danced across the terrain with gentle brushes of refreshing coolness, making each breath an invigorating, revitalizing act; an incredible backdrop for some violently soothing brooding, Harry thought to himself. Melancholy notions drifted in and out of his skull. He felt a kind of misery that was inevitable for all people of his sort, he reflected cooly, and wondered if success, achievement, glory, and notoriety would remedy him of this fraudulent feeling at all, or if these cumbersome moods were simply genetic predispositions, etched in his DNA, impervious to anything tangible and external that the world impressed upon him. A quote flashed through his mind quickly, one that left an imprint on him at a younger age, and it came from a very unlikely source, a movie, with Katharine Hepburn. He couldn't remember the title of the film, for it was not that good a movie, but there was a line that Hepburn uttered, that was profoundly true, Harry thought, and it arose once again in his mind. "Life isn't about getting what you want. It's about wanting it after you get it." When he first heard this line at a tender age, he didn't think too much of it, brushed it off as a very cleverly written line, by a bunch of clever Hollywood writers. For all the writers from Los Angeles in those days, working for Hollywood, were clever. That was their trademark, their purpose, and they were very good at it. The studio executives didn't want them to be anything other than clever. "Save the philosophy and depth for the novel," one studio head was famous for saying, and I'm sure that this line written for Hepburn was not intended to have anything but cleverness running through it, and that the writer was clearly just playing with words, kind of like a jigsaw puzzle, but intention and meaning are two very different things, and sometimes, Harry understood all too well, the so called simplest, most spontaneous, and most playfully executed action, can hold incomparable complexities, and wholly penetrating truths within them.

Would it really matter if I became a great

pianist and composer? Harry thought to himself.

Would I not still enjoy visiting my patio in the late

evening and swimming with my memories and

daydreams? Would I really be content? Is it possible,

for a man with my temperament, to be contented?

Shouldn't the music alone stand on its own merit, for

it's beauty and expression? Rationally and logically

this assuaged Harry's downtroddenness for the time

being, but dreams and aspirations were never

rational. Desires and obsessions were never concrete

and understandable. They always resided on the

supernatural side of things. One could justify anything

with enough philosophizing and ruminating, even

murder, but that doesn't change the implacable

compulsions that invade and dominate one's heart

and mind. So, this ache, this prickling thorn, this

ingratiating urge to attain a place in the pantheon of

the great masters of his art would not leave him be.

Like an obstinate child, his propensity for fame, poked

him, laughed at him, provoked him, and annoyed him

so readily that his identity was lost without it and he

would always carry the feeling of walking in a

charlatan's cloak unless he reached that status. Harry

paused amidst this sequence of thoughts, and beheld

the immense silence that shrouded over him. It was

becoming late in the evening, and his wife was long

gone to bed, as was most of the neighborhood. He

drifted back to his father's funeral, and how quickly it

was completed. The lowering of his body in that

unforgiving Earth, amidst sobs and stoic postures,

flew across his upward gaze. His brandy tasted sour

as he tipped the glass to his lips, and he grimaced,

quickly placing it aside.

He was saddened at how namelessly his father passed through this life. He was saddened at how he never really knew anything about him. He suddenly became intensely curious about what his daily life was occupied with. What was his work like? How did they treat him at work? Did he get along with his co-workers? Did he sit on this porch the same way I do, endlessly wrapped up in his own thoughts? He became acutely aware of the fact that he knew next to nothing about his father, and what he truly thought of his family, his life, his work, his existence. With heartbreaking agony, Harry tried to conjure a conversation, an instance, where him and his father exchanged anything that resembled something of a benign, memorable, good time, a good laugh, a proud

moment, and Harry was at a loss. He was sure there

must have been at least one memory devoid of

disenchantment, contempt, and admonishment, but

Harry helplessly came up empty. The wind became

stronger and more biting against Harry's flesh, as he

started to shake from the intense cold that came with

it. He rose from his seat and headed off to bed.

◆

Harry stood in front of the mirror buttoning up

his shirt, as he heard cars arriving, and feet trampling,

and doors being slammed, with alarms being

activated. The bedroom faced the street over the

garage, and the guests could be heard with great ease as they made their way to the front door. Harry could recognize a few of the voices that arose from the muffled murmurings of conversation. "Did you remember my glasses?" he thought he heard Andy Mulvey say in that distinctly hoarse voice of his.

"Harry, they're here! Hurry up!" he could hear his wife yelling from downstairs. He stepped in front of the mirror in the bedroom which reflected his entire body. A despondent face looked back, as he scrutinized himself for an appropriate appearance, as most people do who have leapt passed the stage of protecting their vanity, with quick, thoughtless movements of adjusting the hair, and attire. He straightened his collar, brushed his pants, was about to walk downstairs, when his eyes caught his zipper

undone, in the reflection, just as he was turning away.

He stammered erect in front of the mirror again,

quickly zipping the open fly, pausing for a moment or

two in that reflection. He wrapped his tongue around

his gums and rubbed his eyes and chin. His skin felt

extraordinarily flaccid and leathery, it struck Harry

unexpectedly. "What are you?" he mumbled to himself

automatically, suddenly terrified upon hearing those

words come out of his mouth, as if he had not said

them, and he was thoroughly disgusted with his

appearance, like he had never seen himself before,

and now suddenly after all these years he was able to

view what horrors lied behind this devilish carcass

that dressed him. He winced slightly and drew himself

back. He felt like his conscience was on full display,

that his darkest secrets were exposed like a front page headline, legible in the folds of wrinkles that adorned his face. He exhaled a sigh and turned away from the mirror resolutely.

The front entrance of the house was teeming with activity as guests made their way in greeted by Harry's wife. "Where is the big guy?" asked one of them.

"He is still getting ready, you know Harry, always late," said his wife with as much lightheartedness as she could muster.

Harry could see his friends entering the house from the top of the stairs, and they all looked up to see him. Big smiles greeted him as he made his way down the staircase that led to the entrance. Harry smeared a smile across his face and cheers and hurrahs were

exhorted from all around. Suddenly, Harry lost his

footing midway down the stairs and tumbled forward,

head first, crashing onto the floor, his body immobile,

and unconscious.

◆

Harry awoke in a hospital bed, as his eyelids languidly

opened, his wife, his son Jerry, and his wife Alice,

were all sitting next to his bed, inside a single room

plastered with the usual, institutional colored

wallpaper and design that always created an

atmosphere of immediacy. Everything gray and cold,

with beeping and chiming instruments positioned

about the room.

"Harry, are you awake?" his wife cried with eyes that were watery, red, and puffy, like someone who had been crying for a long period of time. She stood up and walked closer to the bed.

"Mom, don't crowd him, give him some room," Jerry said. Harry heard the familiar voice fly into the air and it echoed through the hallways of his memory. It sounded so foreign yet familiar at the same time. He was besieged by a series of rapid images that jetted past his eyes: the stairs, the reflection, the immense silence, the zipper, Chopin, Chinese food, sunset, those boots! Perspiration caked his forehead as he motioned, with his hand, that he was thirsty.

"I think he's thirsty," Harry's wife said.

"I'll go get him some water," said Alice. Harry's wife inched closer to him with a paper towel and wiped his forehead and gently caressed his cheek. "Oh Harry, I'm so sorry," she said with a faint whisper. Alice returned with the water and handed it to Harry. He struggled and, aided by his wife, took a long drink and could feel every muscle and bone in his face ache with incredible pain. He put his hand to his temple, out of instinct, and realized that his face was covered in bandages. "What happened?" he said with great effort, quivering, terror filled. He scanned the faces in the room. His wife cast her eyes to the floor, Alice didn't breathe a response, and Jerry looked straight at him, with penetration, stolidly, unwaveringly, and said, "You tripped over your shoelace." Harry froze with disbelief, forlorn, and squashed. "You're lucky to be alive," Jerry added after a pause, with an expression glazed across his face as expressionless as it was effortless; in a tone that betrayed no emotion. A wax figure bore more animate features. He looked like a tree standing impervious to an oncoming brush fire. Jerry's mother began to cry softly, and gradually the sobs became stronger and more voluminous, and violently shook her body. Jerry's steely glare did not soften at all, and remained fixed on Harry. Alice rushed over to console and comfort her. Harry felt limp, and weightless. He struggled to maintain consciousness, and felt his eyes sting with every blink. "Could you guys leave me alone for awhile?" he said with his face directed at the ceiling.

"Come on, let's go and get some coffee," said

Jerry addressing his mother and Alice.

"I want you to stay Jerry," Harry said with such conviction that you would never think that he had just been in an awful accident.

"I think it would be better if you had some rest," Jerry said. "The doctor said–"

"I want you to stay," Harry interrupted. Alice and Jerry's mother left the room after Jerry nodded to them that he was going to comply with Harry's request. He turned back to his father who looked like a peaceful man in the midst of prayer, his hands locked together at his waist, eyes closed, breathing softly, and easy; in a deathly peaceful state.

"I really think I should leave you alone to rest.

You look very tired," Jerry said with trepidation.

Harry lifted his hand toward Jerry, extended his right index finger, opened his eyes, looked at his son, and said, "I'm going to tell you everything."

WALTZING WITH SIN

Cooper walked towards the brown Ford pick up truck, dragging his bulbous linen sack of clothes, aluminum cans, and newspapers draped over his shoulder. Perspiration peppered

his broad forehead. His thin, gaunt body shuffled across the asphalt, with sooted feet dressed in turquoise-green sandals reduced to a slab of credit card thin rubber separating him from the scorching earth. The passenger door opened. The driver was a robust man in middle age. Round, protruding, sky blue eyes greeted Cooper.

"Hop in buddy," the driver said. An inviting smile covered his stubbled face.

"Thank you," said Cooper. He climbed into the passenger seat after placing his things in between him and the driver. The truck ambled down the highway.

"Where you headed?" The driver said.

"Anywhere," said Cooper. He cleared his throat. It was an unusually dry, hot day in Southern California. The Santa Ana winds had engulfed the entire South coast of Orange County, bringing with it all the dust, grime, soot, and heat from the inland valleys. The 133 freeway unraveled itself before Cooper's eyes in blurry, bleary, waves of optical wizardry. The wind broke against his leathery face with as much yearning for quenching as he possessed.

It hadn't rained in over six months. The driver squeezed his eyes together and fixed them on Cooper.

"How did you end up on the highway, buddy?" he inquired. The interior of the truck was rigged with an elaborate array of devices. Communications equipment, highly sensitive radio utilities, and things blinking and whirring with that mechanical sensibility were found adorning the dashboard and roof of the truck. Cooper's muddy brown eyes roamed around the cabin of the truck. "Did you get lost or something?" the driver said with a chuckle.

"Sort of," Cooper said quietly. His eyes darted around in dazzling rapidity resting on a French fry finally that was lying underneath the armrest. He looked up at the driver who was looking ahead. He reached over to grab the French fry slowly, all the while steadying his eyes on the driver. Cooper tried to bite into the fry, but it was solid. He scrunched his face and threw the fry out the open window.

"Well, be careful roaming around these streets, buddy. A lot of conservative types, who don't like anything dirty. I feel the same as most of them, just more honest about it. Bums remind people of the swine that they really are, and they depreciate the community. Nobody likes them kinda reminders, know what I mean?" the driver said shooting a sharp glance over at Cooper. Cooper nodded, eyes swarming the scene. "I've seen a lot of bums in my time, and you look about the worst," he continued. He leaned back in the plastic seat, his head tilted upwards slightly, forearm extended to the wheel, while the other one rested on the window ledge. "You must be new to this area, hey?"

"Naturally," Cooper said. He clenched his hands tightly.

"Whereabouts you from?"

"San Antonio."

"Is that so?" the driver exclaimed. "You're a long ways from home."

Cooper remained stiff, every part of his body, except for his eyes, was fixed in frozen immobility. The driver was wearing white overalls atop a white shirt. Black smudges were found almost everywhere on his person. His pants, shirt, elbows, and hands all bore the marks of a man who worked under the sun, but they didn't look like they belonged there, like most men who are accustomed to dirt. His arms were uncannily smooth. His teeth had met a toothbrush regularly. He slept on clean sheets with a burdenless conscience.

"I used to contract work out in Lubbock," the driver said. "Yeah, I knew you were an out-of-towner," he added after a pause, with lips that remained glassed into a smile. He shifted in his seat and looked out the window. Cooper looked down at his feet, stuck both his hands under his armpits, wrapping his forearms tightly around his waist. The driver sniffed the air in quick increments and looked over at Cooper. Averting his eyes hastily after meeting the driver's glance, Cooper slowly craned his neck towards his underarm, whiffed cautiously two times, slowly lifted his head, looking out the window of swiftly rolling strawberry fields and barren plains. A ringing sound floated in the air from one of the radios. The driver placed a receiver in his hand that connected to the machine with a coiled plastic wire. "Roger that," and "Be there in fifteen," were uttered in between momentary pauses.

"Well, bud, duty calls," the driver said. "I gotta head to North County. I can drop you off at Alton." Passing a large sign that read: Irvine City Limits, the truck exited the freeway and came to a stop at an intersection that had little activity, a few vague buildings on one side and construction taking place on the other. Drilling sounds filled the air. A few shouts from people working on the second storey of one of the buildings to people on the ground level were heard in the distance. The wind gusted hard, filling the air with dust particles. Cooper grabbed his linen bag and exited the truck. He turned toward the driver.

"No need to say thanks," the driver said. "I always try to help you guys out." With a wrinkle in his brow, Cooper stood outside the truck, darting his eyes in unspecific locations. He leaned on the passenger door with his hands folded over the ledge.

"Any chance you need an extra hand?" Cooper said slowly. His eyes lulled on the driver. Shaking his head with a wry smile the driver said, "Sorry bud, but even if I needed an extra guy, in the condition you're in, and the way you smell, I wouldn't be able to take you on. It would be unsanitary, know what I mean?"

Cooper nodded. He raised his hand exposing his palm to the driver. The truck sped off leaving Cooper alone on the street. He turned towards the direction of the construction site. A huge crane transferred boxes from a cargo truck to the skeletal building. He turned back around to the other side of the street. There were two office spaces dressed in large tinted windows, flanked by a vacant parking lot. Thin trees swaying in the wind lined the entrances. An old lady was sitting by herself at a bus stop fifteen yards north of him. The wind roared again, drying his wet patches of hair that wrapped around his pointy chin, ending at his disconnected ear lobes. The sun was in its wane, casting large shadows across the street. Cooper took out a photo from the back pocket of his charcoal gray jeans. A woman with chestnut hair, a trim figure, and a small child meeting her at the waist, with blonde curls and a bright red ski jacket were standing in the foreground of two Emerald trees staring back at him. He placed the photo back in his pocket, picked up his bag and walked down Alton parkway. The winds provided him with a penetrating waft of the smell he exuded. The driver's nose twitching face flashed across his eyes for a moment. With the exception of the few automobiles flying past him, the surroundings changed very little. Cooper walked for two miles. Within that stretch he experienced nothing bustling with heavy life. Every building he approached had little to no contrast from the structures he had passed along the way. Signs that read, 'Business District', or 'Business Parkway', were ubiquitously placed in front of the commonly black tinted edifices with empty parking lots, and withered clumps of greenery dressing the walkways.

Cooper sat down at a dull green colored bench with a large placard on the back rest advertising a hip hop radio show. Night swallowed the sky gradually. He stretched out his legs, raising them a few inches off the ground when a voice came from behind him.

"You're almost there," a hoarse voice said. Cooper swiftly turned around and saw nobody. He felt a hand grab his ankle. He jumped out of his seat and hurriedly grabbed his bag, eyes shifting like a pendulum. "I know what you want," the voice said again.

Cooper ran without turning back. He slowed to a walk after he had distanced himself a hundred yards from the bench, panting, trying to catch his breath. His ears burned with an intense stabbing pain shooting through his temples. He cupped his hands around them, standing still, grimacing. A ringing filled the inside of his ears and mind. The cars that flew by him did so without warning. Cooper stuck his index finger inside his ear and shook the cartilage violently. The intensity of the pain subsided slowly. The ringing waned after ten minutes had passed.

As he was walking he noticed some flashes of color in his peripheral vision. He turned obliquely to his left, towards the road, and there was a police

squad car with its red and blue lights dancing upon

his face, rolling along with Cooper's pace. Cooper gave

a start, and stopped walking. The squad car mimicked

his movements and halted on the shoulder of the

road. Cooper stiffened; his eyes roaming the entire

globe, a faint whisper rose to his ears and slowly

became louder. He walked towards the passenger side

door of the vehicle. A giant, completely bald head,

with a bushy mustache draped over the upper lip was

mouthing to him forcefully. The heat in his ears

cooled to a warm glow. Everything showered upon

Cooper in stereo sound abruptly as he lowered his

head down to meet the officer's gaze.

"Can you understand what I am saying?" the

officer yelled. A shotgun was holstered in the divide between the driver and passenger seats. Its elongated barrel almost reached the ceiling of the car, a prominent fixture in the foreground of Cooper's point of view. Cooper jerked his neck back, pursing his lips, eyes scanning up, down, east, and west. "I have been honking at you for the past five minutes," the officer said. His skin bare head gave him the appearance of being a mature man, but his eyes were young, fierce, and bore no signature wrinkles under them to denote aging. His face was pale, clean, unblemished. "You on something?" the officer continued. Cooper stood motionless. The smell of rubber emanated from the passenger window. The officer opened his driver side door and exited the vehicle maintaining a stern look on his face.

"What's your name buddy?" the officer demanded while walking toward Cooper on the other side of the car with a flashlight in his hand. "If you're trying be smart with me, I'm gonna tell you right now, that ain't the way to go." Cooper felt electric heat course through his limbs, his throat strained to swallow, his mouth made a Velcro sound when his lips parted and compressed, from the excessive dryness.

The officer was dressed in all black with padding on his shoulders. He was tall, with a broad chest and a thick neck. On each side of his hips were two .38 specials holstered on his belt, along with a baton, can of mace, a Cold Steel Gunsight edition military knife, and a walkie talkie that blared out arbitrary phrases now and then. A 9mm pistol was strapped to his right thigh and long, knee high, black commando boots finished the outfit. Cooper squeezed his eyes tightly in response to the beam of light magnified on his face.

"Jesus almighty... you look like day old trash," the officer said, almost to himself, after scanning, with the flashlight, up and down Cooper's body. Shivering, Cooper cast his eyes to the ground. "Good god, what the hell is that smell?" the officer shouted, covering his mouth with his free hand. He backed away from Cooper several feet, coughing and spitting onto the sidewalk. "You stay right there!" the officer yelled, standing by the rear of the vehicle, still spitting. Cooper raised his eyes, wrapped his arms around his abdomen tightly, burying his hands underneath his underarms. He moved his tongue around his moistless mouth, which instigated a cough that lasted a few seconds. The officer, still covering his mouth, walked back over to the driver side door of the police vehicle.

"Have a seat on the curb for me," the officer said, pointing his finger south. Cooper remained immobile, eyes frozen on the ground. After a few moments he sat himself down on the curb, a few feet away from the rear of the car. The emergency lights splashed across his quivering body noiselessly.

Cooper could hear the officer blow his nose several times. He saw him approach from the driver's side of the car.

"Alright buddy what's going on?" the officer said. Cooper looked up at the policeman, who was standing directly in front of him. "What do you call yourself? You got a name?"

"Cooper."

"Ok, Cooper, are you physically, or mentally hurt or ill in any way?" the officer said, pointing his flashlight directly into Cooper's face. Cooper adjusted his knees in front of his chest, resting his folded arms on them, looking down. "It's okay, we're just talking here Cooper. You're not in any trouble. I just want to help. You're going to have to be honest with me, so that I can do that to the best of my ability."

Cooper slowly looked up and said, "I'm just a little hungry."

"When was the last time you ate?" the officer said.

"Yesterday," Cooper said.

"Yesterday, hey?" the officer spoke, eyeing Cooper closely. "Well, I would be pretty hungry too, If I hadn't eaten for twenty four hours." After placing the end of the flashlight through his arm, the officer took out a pad and pen and began writing.

"Remember who you're dealing with," a voice uttered, that seemed to come from the sky. It spoke with such roughness, with such eerie directness, that Cooper stood up immediately, shaking, looking in every direction.

"Hey, sit down Cooper, we're not quite done

yet," The officer said, motioning to the floor with his hand. Cooper did not hear him. A terribly fierce shiver overcame him. His breathing was rapid, his eyes enlarged, reality quickly flushed from his cheeks. He felt an extreme need to flee, to run and run only, without restraint, without purpose. "Take it easy, buddy," the officer spoke, while grabbing Cooper by the arms. "It's gonna be alright. I'm trying to help you," the officer said, failing to suppress his indignation.

"Please let me go," Cooper said, with a cracked voice.

"Where are you gonna go? Do you even have a place to go to? I'm not the enemy, ok? Listen, buddy, this is my city, and I have to keep it safe. I am responsible for upholding order. And by the looks of you, order, is something that's missing badly. Now take a seat, and let's work this out."

Cooper slowly sat back down on the curbside, after a few more coughs. With his hands shaking, he flopped his head over his raised knees.

"Cooper...you're going to have to talk to me," the officer said.

Cooper raised his head. He looked towards the traffic that was flowing more frequently, headlights swarming by, one after the other. He then looked up at the officer like a cornered poodle, submissively, dejectedly.

"How did you get this way?" the officer asked.

Cooper stayed quiet. The officer did not flinch. After having his head down for what seemed an eternity, Cooper looked up at the stolid man.

"I'm not sure I understand..." Cooper spoke slowly.

"Yes you do," the officer shoved in quickly. Cooper averted his eyes. "Unless you have no recollection, which would force me to believe that you are ill, and therefore justify my taking you in for the proper care you need. But you don't want that do you?" the officer added emphasizing the last word. "Do you?" he repeated louder than before.

Cooper shook his head slowly, bouncing his knees, lifting his heel swiftly, underneath folded arms.

"Reveal nothing!" the haunting, raspy voice echoed. Cooper pressed his eyelids together vigorously, swaying his curled body on the curb back and forth frantically.

"Ok Cooper, you leave me no choice, stand up," the officer said.

"I have a place to go," Cooper said suddenly, with exasperation, raising his shaky hand, swiftly rising to his feet.

"Too late Cooper, you had your chance."

"Please officer, you don't understand," Cooper said, standing up quickly. "I have a job to do."

"You have a job?" the officer said incredulously.

"Yes, I just need to get to North County."

"Where in North County?"

"I'm not sure exactly, I am meeting my foreman on Alton," Cooper said.

"You're on Alton," the officer spoke in a low voice, sniffing several times, clearing his throat. Cooper backed away from him slightly, folding his arms tight.

"I'm supposed to meet him here soon," Cooper offered.

"At this time of night? Come on, Cooper."

"Honestly officer," Cooper said with large breaths, "He should be here any minute." The officer took a few moments to look Cooper over.

"You go to work in that condition?" the officer

said.

"There are locker rooms on site."

"Site?"

"Yes, the work site," Cooper fumbled quickly.

"What kind of work?"

"Construction," Cooper said.

"You must take me for a real idiot," the officer said dramatically, slowly moving his head up and down. "You think I'm dumb? Are you calling an officer of the law a fool?"

Cooper furrowed his brow, slumping backward. "Honestly, officer....I .... would never..."

"You know there comes a time when it becomes

too much to take," the officer spoke exhaling big. "All the lies, the filth, the waste."

Cooper felt stricken by something, clutched his legs, standing tensely erect. Never ceasing with his eyes, Cooper dared to flash a quick look up at the officer who became pensive and silent. The officer, with his hands on his hips, looked pale, with eyes that no longer resided in real time. The policeman stayed implacable. Cooper felt a weight on his chest.

"You're lucky I don't want my squad car to smell like urine, or you would be coming with me," the officer said abruptly. Cooper bowed his head.

The officer eyed Cooper's bag. "Let me guess, you got your work tools, and things in the bag?" the officer said, narrowing his eyes back on Cooper.

"Yes."

"I don't have to search that thing do I?"

"I only have my work clothes, and miscellaneous things," Cooper said in a hushed tone, bubbles of perspiration forming on his face.

"Nothing illegal in there right? No Drugs, contraband, or weapons of any kind?"

"No," Cooper said quietly.

"Okay. Give me your identification and that will be our last order of business," the policeman said with resolution.

Cooper sluggishly stepped back, bending his gaze to the ground, with trembling shoulders.

"Well?" the officer said impatiently.

"I don't have it."

"You're making this really hard Cooper."

Cooper didn't stir. Walking back towards his vehicle, the officer spat on the pavement, opened the door, paused, and looked over at Cooper. "Don't make me look bad Cooper. I'm trusting you. If I see you again and find out you lied, you can guarantee that all the kindness I have shown you will be thrown out the window."

The officer pointed his fore-finger at Cooper threateningly, lowered his body into the driver's seat and drove away. Cooper stood in the same spot on the sidewalk watching the black and white car recede into a tiny speck, turn left around a corner and disappear.

Cooper felt a tug on his shoulder by a swift palm that effortlessly shook his whole body around. Again, his roving eyes revealed no figure present.

Cooper turned in all directions, wild eyed, feeling an acute coldness cover his body. Almost immediately he felt a warmth inch up his arms. A minute calm came over him. What he just felt seemed like it was something wholly disconnected from himself, miles away, like a drifting comet. The stars revealed themselves in the blackened sky as Cooper ran his hands through his hair, grabbed the waist of his jeans and pulled them up with a gentle tug, straightened his posture by arching his back, and raised his shoulders up. He passed the tip of his tongue over his lips.

Picking up his sack, Cooper rounded a corner that led to a residential area. Rows of two-storey houses lined the street with tiny front lawns that consisted of sparse flowers and shrubs. The amber glow of the street lights bathed the neighborhood in a coppery tinge. Other than a few doors being shut and faint barks from dogs echoing through the air, a pervasive stillness overcame the neighborhood. His nostrils enlarged, a waft of deliciousness assailed him. He could smell the aroma of peppered steak that almost leveled his weary body. He closed his eyes, deeply inhaled, and then slowly exhaled. He tried to swallow some saliva that had built up in his mouth, but this only led to more coughing. His esophagus was coarse and inflamed. The air continued its reign of dry gusts saturated with dust.

He walked down the street which led to a clearing. A large field of grass adjacent to a sand patch with a volleyball net stood before him. He noticed a sign made of wood that read, Royal Oak Park that preceded a tiny parking lot on his right hand side. A swimming pool was centered in the middle surrounded by an iron gate. An elderly woman was walking a small dog through the open terrain. Cooper walked towards the playground with downcast eyes. A jungle gym, swing set, and a large, coiling, tube slide with a connecting arched bridge to another wave slide made up the child's play ground which sat underneath a large Walnut tree. A street light flickered on and off rapidly, producing a strobe light effect. Cooper stopped suddenly, walked to a water fountain near the entrance of the swimming pool, pushed the circular metal knob, and refreshed himself with some cold water. He drank with such vigor that he nearly choked himself. The cool water mingled violently with his parched throat. The first breath after raising his head from the faucet caused him to cough loudly. He wiped his mouth with his forearm, placed his hand on his chest, and breathed deeply. He tasted a hint of blood on the top of his tongue after swallowing several times. He shuddered. He looked around with swift eyes. The lady with the dog was no longer around. The sounds of crickets, night critters, the incessant buzz of the street lamps, and muffled barks from dogs far in the distance, were the only signs that Cooper was not alone. He felt a sudden wave of fatigue blanket his body. He scanned around the park. He noticed a large, plastic, rectangular shaped block of some sort underneath the vertical ladder leading to the slide entrance on the playground with a large opening and bubble windows on its side panels, big enough to hold a couple of eight year olds. He walked to it, sat upright inside, with his feet dangling out onto the soft surface, closed his eyes, and immediately fell asleep.

He awoke three hours later to a faint plucking of strings accompanied by a soft, raspy voice. He lifted his head with lighting speed, chewing the air with his roving eyes. Am I still dreaming? He asked himself. He shook the lingering slumber of sleep off, slowly peeked out of his plastic shelter, and saw a tiny figure, silhouetted by the street light, with his back facing him, sitting on a swing, with a guitar on his lap.

Cooper narrowed his eyes, craned his neck, and bent his ear in the direction of the melody. The voice traversed the air with splendid ease. The night air seemed to cuddle the words coming out of his mouth, welcoming the song with open arms. The chiming of the crickets subdued respectfully, the murmurings of the neighborhood came to a halt. Cooper remained still. These words sailed to his ears:

Someday you'll find that the world left you out

No true love, no nothing, just roaming about

Wild parties and people, and a cold heart within

And each time you're dancing, you're waltzing with sin

Cooper leaned back, suspended his breath, eyes closed, shifting his head from side to side in time with the song, with very little movement. The voice grasped the words with a sense of ownership, sitting in between them with perfect hesitation, uttering without haste, pausing poignantly when appropriate; allowing the melody to gain its momentum effortlessly. Cooper sat in the same spot. His body leaned towards the dark figure. He placed his hand on his chest, adjusted his legs in front of him, and unburdened his shoulders. Cooper smiled a private smile.

The words trailed off and the boy struck the strings slowly one by one then came to a stop. Cooper lifted himself up, drew a deep breath, widening his dancing eyes. The spark of a cough inflamed his throat vehemently. He tried to suppress it by holding his breath, but to no avail. He coughed violently, tasting small traces of blood on the top of his sandpaper tongue. A long period of time had passed since a sizable amount of oxygen filled his chest. The unprepared lungs heaved uncontrollably. The boy started, sprang to his feet, turned towards Cooper with a bewildered hare's speed.

"Who goes there?" the boy said, taking a few steps back. Cooper raised his hand, extended his index finger, coughing in an incessant bout that didn't seemed to relent, trying to catch his breath.

"I apologize," Cooper said wheezingly. "I didn't mean to scare you." The silhouette did not stir.

"Who are you?" the boy asked.

"I'm a harmless nobody."

Cooper stood up. He looked at the boy, realized how small he was, comparatively. It was too dark to make out a face, but Cooper measured, by the size of his shoulders and overall stature, that he was no bigger than a teenager, standing at about five feet and four inches. His voice sounded like it was in the throes of puberty; not quite adolescent, but years from maturation.

The whirring from the street lamp penetrated the silence that ensued for as long as it takes to tie a shoe. Cooper bent over, placed his hands on his knees, and coughed some more, each succeeding cough less harsh than the previous.

"What are you doing out here?" the boy said.

"I was just trying to get some rest," Cooper said while pounding his chest with his closed hand. "That was beautiful what you were playing," Cooper said, after regrouping on the floor directly in front of the swing set. The boy stood behind the swing, guitar tucked under his right arm. "Did you write that yourself?"

"No... it's an old song..." The boy said looking down, kicking the sand gently with his foot, swaying his shoulders mildly. "You heard me sing?" the boy said, raising his head.

"Yes, I did," Cooper responded. "I hope you don't mind?" Cooper placed his hands underneath his armpits, elbows resting across his chest. The boy shook his head slowly. Another silence.

"Are you a hobo?" the boy inquired. Cooper gave a start, declined his gaze. "There are a lot of songs about hobos," the boy added quickly, with an octave higher than before. The boy lowered himself onto the swing.

"Would you play me one?" Cooper asked.

The boy shuffled his feet, looked at his guitar, then cast his eyes to the ground, and said, "I don't know any by heart." Cooper nodded his head slowly. The boy placed the guitar on its back on the sand. "I've never seen anybody out here this late before," the boy said.

"What time is it?" Cooper asked. Looking at his watch,

the boy offered, "It's one forty five." Cooper's

eyebrows rose. The boy swung his legs, that didn't

touch the ground, to and fro underneath the swing. He

took out a pack of Dunhill Reds from his right side

jacket pocket. He offered one to Cooper. Cooper shook

his head, indicating his throat with his finger. "I guess

that was stupid of me," the boy said with a strained

laugh. The boy took out a silver Zippo lighter

that reflected the dim street light, lit his cigarette,

extended his right hand toward Cooper, while

placing the Zippo, with his left hand, back in his

pocket. "I'm Stanley."

A faint waft of butane filled the air momentarily.

Cooper extended his hand then quickly retracted it,

placing it behind his back. Stanley slowly lowered his

stretched arm. A wry smile played on his face.

"I'm Cooper."

"Nice to meet you," Stanley said.

Stanley picked up the guitar, rested it on his lap, and started strumming some random chords. His cigarette dangled from his lips. He stopped playing, took a long drag, the red glow from the end brightening with each puff, rested his elbow on the body of the guitar, and looked over at Cooper with his chin buried in his hand.

"I'm just taking a wild guess here, but something tells me you're from a far away place." Stanley quickly struck a few notes on the guitar.

"I've been getting that a lot lately," Cooper

responded. A breeze brushed against Cooper's face, producing a chill that ran up his neck. The gust manifested a cooler note to it. A thin mist descended on the playground. Cooper closed his eyes, flared his nostrils drawing a long breath, leaning his head back, his chest expanding, looking towards the sky. The cool air floated through his larynx sweetly, creating a soothing balm to his sore airway.

"I feel like I'm from a far away place," Stanley uttered almost inaudibly. He picked a little louder, a sharp twang rising in the air. He desisted unexpectedly. Taking another drag from

his grit, he raised his eyes to meet Cooper's. "You gotta get out of this place," Stanley said in a forceful whisper.

"Why is that?"

"Why?" Stanley repeated incredulously, furrowing his eyebrows, his eyes narrowing to small slits. He stood up from the swing, almost threw the guitar on the floor, turned his back on Cooper, and faced the neighborhood, professing, almost in a yell, "Just take a look around this abomination. It's filled with nothing, absolutely nothing." With a flourish of his right arm he added, "Every single house is the same, every car is the same, every idea that floats in and out of the heads of these detestable wretches is the same. They all look the same. There is nothing fresh, new, or original...nothing--" he trailed off, stopping suddenly, back still turned on Cooper. Stanley exhaled, turned around, and fell into the swing, with his head bent down. Cooper sat

motionless. "I'm sorry," Stanley murmured, without

turning his face towards Cooper. He searched his vest

pocket, pulled out another Dunhill, and lit it.

"It's ok," Cooper said. Stanley puffed away,

voluptuous smoke steaming slowly from his mouth,

caressing his cheeks, looking away from Cooper,

facing the neighborhood. "How long have you lived

here?" Cooper said after a lengthy pause.

"Too long," Stanley answered. Cooper sat still, head

bowed towards the ground, hands clasped together,

resting on his thighs. "As soon as I can get a real job,

and earn enough dough, I'm outta here," Stanley

pronounced emphatically, in a breathless whisper,

meditating on each word, uttering the last three with

a histrionic flare, almost like he was talking to himself.

Cooper turned his face away from Stanley. A smile

consumed his face.

"You've got that bug," Cooper said, looking

away.

"What do you mean? What bug?"

"The only bug that matters. The one that drives

us all to do things we can't avoid doing. You got it

sooner than most."

"Is that a good thing or a bad thing?" Stanley

asked, smoking away. Cooper hesitated a moment,

tilting his head slightly, curling his lips in and out.

"It doesn't matter," Cooper said, looking up,

"You have to deal with it either way."

"How do you deal with it?"

"Just like you're doing."

"By getting angry?" Stanley said, squishing his face together.

"There's nothing wrong with getting angry," Cooper calmly retorted, "sometimes anger is exactly what's needed."

"That's not what they tell me," Stanley said, looking intently at Cooper. Cooper smiled. "But I feel like you're right." Cooper let out a long breath.

"If I'm so right, then--"

"I have to go to this bullshit EFT class three nights a week, and my Mom wants to put me on levetiracetam," Stanley said, not hearing Cooper.

"What's EFT?" Cooper asked. Stanley shook his head, forced a smile, and grunted a few times.

"Emotional Freedom Techniques." They both looked at each other with oblique expressions. After a moment they burst into laughter. Cooper coughed forcefully, grabbing his throat with one hand, while the other laid flat on his chest. "You see why I gotta get the hell

outta here?" Stanley added, still laughing. Cooper spit out onto the ground a few times, clearing his throat loudly. He grunted approvingly to Stanley.

"Everything seems to make me mad," Stanley said, more solemnly, taking his Zippo out to light another Dunhill, drawing the smoke deep into his lungs, "People just aren't good to each other."

"Just make sure you get it out," Cooper said, breathing easier.

"Get what out?"

"The bug."

"What if I don't?" Stanley said.

"You will."

"How do you know?"

"Because it will bug you till you do," Cooper said.

"Can I kill it?" Stanley asked.

"No."

"Can it kill me?"

"Yes."

"Did it kill you?" Stanley asked, with slight hesitation, in a low voice.

Cooper shuddered, dashing here, there, everywhere, with his butterfly eyes.

Gripping, with his free hand, one of the two chains holding the swing up, while leaning back slightly looking around at everything, then resting on Cooper, Stanley said, "This can't be what they envisioned. Is this their paradise? Fucking Starbucksland?" Stanley turned his head for a moment giving a profile view to Cooper. The back light showed Stanley's large nose which protruded upward with continuous concavity from the eyes to the tip. "What brought you this way?" Stanley said, after taking a long drag from his cigarette.

"Carelessness."

"What were you careless about?" Stanley added after a moment.

Cooper looked up at Stanley for a moment then bowed his head back down to the floor. "Everything," he said with a tremor in his voice. The sound of sizzling tobacco, mingled with the suction sound of Stanley's lips as they parted from the cigarette with each drag, dominated the playground.

"What about you?" Cooper said, raising his eyes.

"I've lived here all my life," Stanley said, pointing his free hand vaguely to some houses beyond the large field. "I like to come here and brood when everyone else has gone to bed. I'm a notorious brooder," Stanley said, with a little laugh.

"You must come here a lot, yea?"

Stanley drew another drag from his Dunhill, then placed it atop his clasped thumb and ring finger, launching it a good distance with a flick, where its trailing crimson glow extinguished into the misty night.

"Yeah...it's the only place I can go to," Stanley said, his silhouette refraining from movement, "Everything around here closes at ten o' clock."

"It's a good thing I found this place," Cooper said with a slight shiver that convulsed his shoulders. "It's nice."

"My dad doesn't like me coming here this late,

but it's one of the few places I can go to be alone, and get some peace."

"I can feel that," Cooper said, stretching his arms up in the air. "The whole town seems pretty peaceful."

"This town is nothing, absolutely nothing. That's why it's so quiet," Stanley said, raising his voice slightly, kicking the sand on the playground floor with his shoes that revealed themselves to actually be boots. "All you have is roads and highways paved with lemming commuters, greedy landowners, and itchy cops, with nowhere to scratch. Anybody who tries to break the line get's nothing and has to bleed for survival. It's sometimes too quiet. Too much to take."

"I had a run in with a cop not too long before I

came here," Cooper said, while gathering clumps of sand in his hand and letting it slip out slowly between his semi-closed fist.

"Did he hassle you?"

"Yeah, a little, but he wasn't that bad. I really can't blame them," Cooper said, looking himself over with rapid moving eyes, "I might do the same thing if I looked at the world with their eyes."

"That's just it!" Stanley almost shrieked, making his prepubescence sound like a wounded crow, whining to the unforgivable, indifferent night. "It's a mentality thing with this place, and it goes all the way up and down the line." Stanley became very animated. He stood up abruptly, giving a start to Cooper, who was accustomed to his statuesque rigidity on that swing for so long that the sudden movement contrasted violently. "This place is too safe, there's not enough happening, and it sparks nothing but anxiousness and restlessness. Everyone is itchy! Not just the cops." Cooper shivered again, with his head bowed, hearing everything Stanley said, who was pacing back and forth behind the swing set making lively movements with his arms and shoulders. "They designed this place for comfort and peace, when in fact, it does the opposite." Stanley paused, looking over at Coopers bent figure on the sand. He noticed Cooper's shoulders oscillating slightly. "There's only room for those who have no burden of spirit," he uttered with finality, slouching his shoulders, walking back to the swing where he sat before. A silence permeated everything once again.

Cooper did not change positions, laughed a short, hearty laugh, and said, to the ground beneath him, "You've thought about this a lot."

"I have plenty of time for thoughts," Stanley replied, "as you can see, I don't sleep very much."

"Be thankful that you have youth along with your youthless mind," Cooper remarked looking straight into the dark face of that young shadow. "You have a chance."

"To get rid of the bug?" Stanley said, with a large smile.

"Absolutely."

The thin promise of dawn arose in the sky above them, patches of blue appearing at the edge of the horizon. A loud sound filled the air like a long piece of sketching paper being torn slowly. Cooper looked up at Stanley with a smile, then down at his stomach. Stanley's eyes grew round.

"Wait right here," Stanley said, placing his guitar back in its case, and clasping the brass locks.

"Where are you going?" Cooper inquired, remaining on the sandy floor.

"I'm gonna get something for that monster living in your stomach," Stanley said, with a smile, "I'll be right back. Don't go anywhere."

Stanley rushed off the playground, while Cooper watched him recede into the neighborhood. The street in front of him bore more cars than before, as the morning light was eking across the sky. People

going to work, Cooper assumed. A couple of people

were jogging down the sidewalk, with that look that

joggers have: impervious, stern, pre-occupied.

Nobody noticed Cooper sitting in the middle of the

playground, with both feet bent inwards and under

the body, crossing each other at the ankle. Noticing

that it was becoming less and less dark, the red sun

was rising at a steady pace, Cooper stood up and

walked back to the plastic block where he first heard

the rumblings of Stanley's song, which faced away

from the neighborhood, entered it, and waited. After a

few minutes Cooper fell into a deep sleep.

◆

Cooper lifted his weary eyelids to a man kicking

him lightly by his shins, which were exposed, lying outside the block. He sat up, his eyes stinging when he tried to open them.

"Hey you," the man said, who looked to be slightly elderly, wearing a sweat suit, nudging Cooper with his white tennis shoes, "This is no place to sleep, ya hear?" Cooper didn't move, even though he was fully awake at that moment. "This is a community playground, not a shelter," the man continued. "You get out of there, or I will call the authorities." Cooper came to himself after hearing the last word, and slowly ejected himself from the block. He stood at eye level with the old man. Over his shoulder he could see an elderly woman, with a small girl, sitting at one of the benches that bordered the playground, looking at him with absorption.

"Hey, leave him alone!" was heard coming from the large grassy field. Stanley came running towards them, with a plastic grocery bag in one of his hands. Everyone turned to look at him. As he approached nearer, Cooper saw, for the first time, the shadowy figure, that he conversed with throughout the misty night, unveiled, unmasked, unroofed, under that cloudless sky, of penetrating azure. He looked like a young Indiana Jones from the movies, like some time portal had plopped him down from the sky in the center of that enormous grassy-green patch of Earth. He wore a black leather, fighter pilots jacket, over a beige safari shirt with two flap-closed chest pockets. Suspenders connecting to a hundred percent Twill slacks with outward facing pleats of a coffee with cream, muddy color. And atop his head, sat a wool felt, dark brown, Stetson hat. Cooper stood in vexation for a few moments at the sight of Stanley's rushing, panting figure, and forgot about the old man altogether. With fierce, beady, mossy green eyes, Stanley accosted the old man.

"What's the problem here? Why are you harassing this poor man?" Stanley spoke, with an unrestrained fury. Cooper's eyes stayed on Stanley steady like, with suspended breath.

"Young man, do you know this vagrant?" the old man said.

"Yes I do, and he is not a vagrant. Can't you see he is simply a man resting?"

"Well, he smells like a vagrant and he can't sleep here. This is a children's playground, and my granddaughter wants to play."

"He wasn't sleeping here, he was waiting for me," Stanley yelled.

"Well you're here, so get out of here, before I call the police."

"You can't just ask nicely and be decent about it, can you?" Stanley said bringing his face closer to the old man's chin. He was a lot taller than Stanley. A sharp pain stabbed Cooper in his ears. He placed his hand on his forehead. His legs became very weak. He leaned on the vertical ladder for support, because his thin body began to reel slightly. The pain passed away as quickly as it came, leaving Cooper wrapped in a blanket of disorientation that was felt throughout his limbs. His eyes never left Stanley.

"Young man, I'm warning you," said the old man, contorting his face somewhat. Stanley eased back from the old man a few feet, while internally remaining furious, the folds of his youthful face legibly distressed. He looked over at Cooper, then over at the old lady with the kid on the bench and back to Cooper, who shook his head slowly, with small movements. Cooper grabbed Stanley's right arm above the elbow.

"Alright fine, have your fun, jerk," Stanley said over his shoulder, as he walked away from the old man. "Come on Cooper, let's get outta here."

Before turning away and joining Stanley,

Cooper looked over at the old lady with the little girl and said, "Sorry."

Stanley had walked a good ways before Cooper caught up to him, who had a clean cigarette in between his trembling fingers and mumbling to himself angrily. Cooper noticed, for the first time, walking next to him, how young Stanley looked.

"You see that?" Stanley said curtly, "Fucking asshole. Their everywhere Cooper, I'm telling ya. All over the fucking place ... One slight disturbance in their tedious, routine, boring lives, and they lash out like a bunch of fascists. They can't bear to experience anything out of their normal, phony lives."

"He just wanted his granddaughter to be happy," Cooper said, with eyes bouncing around, "I am pretty atrocious." Stanley looked at Cooper. It seemed that through the whole ordeal with the old man he hadn't really given any attention to Cooper's appearance or condition at all. With that, and the entire evening prior, this was the first time for Stanley to get a clearer glimpse of him. He looked up and down Cooper's person slowly as they walked down the street.

"That still doesn't excuse him for being an asshole," Stanley said, in a quieter voice. Cooper nodded his head, folding his arms, walking briskly beside Stanley on the sidewalk that adorned the same street that led him into the park.

"Where are we going?" Cooper asked.

"Somewhere we won't run into any assholes."

"Is that likely?"

"Probably not," Stanley said, with a grin that turned into a light laugh. Cooper joined him and laughed with his mouth closed making swift, quick breaths, through his nose, that produced barely audible whistling sounds. Stanley's attempt at suppressing his laughter was evident in his trembling, pursed lips. Gradually after a few moments, Stanley's efforts were in vain, and they both laughed out loud.

A bronze Mercedes Benz 500 S screeched to a halt a few feet in front of them, almost clipping the curbside. The automatic passenger side window rolled down and a man's voice shouted from within.

"Stanley! What the hell are you doing," said the driver.

"Oh shit," said Stanley.

"Get over here NOW!"

"Who's that?" asked Cooper. Stanley shoved the bulging, plastic grocery bag into Cooper's hands.

"I gotta go," Stanley said quickly, looking piercingly at Cooper. "Meet me tonight, same bat time, same bat channel." A loud honk blared from the car. Stanley ran to the passenger side, opened it to some imperceptible shouting, sat in, and took off.

The hot, arid, weather had accumulated as the sun made its afternoon ascent. Stanley looked inside the grocery bag, which was filled with an entire roll of French bread, a block of Monterey Jack cheese, two peach flavored Snapple Ice Teas, and a couple of oatmeal cookies wrapped in cellophane. He grabbed

one of the Snapple's, opened it quickly, and drank half

of the sixteen ounce bottle in one gulp, then twisted

the metal cap back on the top. After a few grating

coughs, he wrapped the plastic bag up with his hand

and placed it into his giant linen sack, threw it over

his shoulder and started walking.

The sun pounded on Cooper's brow, causing his

neck and armpits to moisten with sweat. He walked

down the street, head bent to the road. He

approached the intersection, seeing the large soil

colored sign hanging from the streetlight reading,

ALTON PKWY. He looked to the east, then to the west.

Nothing appealing on both sides. Nothing contrasting,

nothing that appeared to be an alternative. He headed

east, turned the right hand corner and noticed

another dull green bench, its metal frame glistening

from the unimpeded sun, with a large trash receptacle

sitting adjacent to it. A flash of that hoarse voice, with

that ominous warning rushed to his ears, and he

shuddered. He stood still, eyes rocketing in all

directions, in the middle of the sidewalk, with the

moistless air perusing his attire. A small, barking,

frantic, Chihuahua, brought him out of his reverie,

nipping at his feet. He looked down at the dog,

followed the black, leather leash up to a lady, with an

iron jaw line, dark eyebrows, and penetrating black

eyes, staring suspiciously and a bit contemptuously,

Cooper thought, at him. Cooper looked at the dog and

smiled, then looked up at the lady and forced another

one for her, quickly turned away and headed down

the road, passing the bench without giving it as much as a sidelong glance.

Cars flew passed him speedily, sending gusts of dry, dusty, debris filled tail winds blowing through his oily, clumped hair, and quickly caking sweat and dirt on his unkempt head. A long, yellow, school bus rushed by him, with the cackle of small children drifting out of the open windows. A little boy yelled at him, "Hey you!" Cooper didn't acknowledge it, and kept his head downcast, walking on, feebly, with quick, little steps. The tree lined street opened to a row of nondescript buildings framing both sides of ALTON, faceless, nameless, covered head to toe with glass panels, shimmering in the sunlight. Cars were entering and exiting the small driveways leading into the basements of the buildings. Cooper came upon a sign that read: IRVINE SPECTRUM, in white lettering on a green background with a white arrow pointing up, underneath. He trudged on.

A vast parking lot with many vacant spaces, fenced in by a neatly groomed hedge loomed ahead of Cooper's ambling figure. Beyond that a large glittering, electric sign, with red, yellow, and green bulbs flashed, CHEESECAKE FACTORY, with a valet directly in front of a patio, where people sat at tables, eating lunch. Directly across the valet was a FOX SPORTS GRILL,

and rising in between these two, a large Ferris wheel revolved slowly with people standing in a line at the ground level. An intersection separated the parking lot from the restaurants. Cooper walked into the parking lot, sat down on one of the

concrete wheel stops, in the shade of a small tree,

opened the grocery bag, and ate voraciously.

A white pick up truck, with yellow flashing lights on

the roof, and big black letters reading: IRVINE

SPECTRUM SECURITY rolled into the parking lot

while Cooper was

finishing his last piece of French bread folded over

slabs of cheese. The driver looked robust, wearing a

black hat with a yellow colored inscription reading:

SECURITY, with his thick arm dangling out of the

driver side window. Cooper looked down at his feet as

the truck circled the parking lot a few times. He rolled

up the empty grocery bag as gently as he could in the

palm of his hand, trying to look casual. He looked up

for a moment, when the vehicle was near; meeting the stern face of the driver, then quickly looked away. The truck circled one more time, then exited the lot.

Cooper stood up, wiped the breadcrumbs from his chest, watching them tumble to the concrete below. The sun beating down on him, coupled with the hearty amount of food residing in his belly made his limbs feel weary, his spirit fatigued. He felt a strong shove behind him, like that of two palms causing him to fall to the ground.

"Remember everything," screeched through the air, in a static, voluminous voice. Cooper tremulously staggered up, seeing nothing around him but empty parking spots and lifeless trees. He ran wildly out of the parking lot back down Alton with furious pace, adrenalin surging through his thighs, an unfounded fear coursing through his veins. People on the sidewalk shrieked when seeing Cooper dash so violently past them. A man shouted, "Hey! What the hell is the rush?" Impervious, Cooper ran for almost a mile. Upon reaching a residential area, Cooper slowed his pace, panting, wheezing, and coughing. He turned onto a street that looked familiar.

This must be it, Cooper thought to himself as he walked down the street, with the familiar houses and light posts dressing both sides. Languidly he made his way to another clearing, the large field and swimming pool jogged his memory. The jungle gym and large Walnut tree stood before him. Something about them didn't seem right. With heavy eyes and exhaustion plastered all over his body, he walked onto the playground. Is this the same place? Cooper thought to himself. The entire park was vacant except for a few gardeners with leaf blowers on the far end.

Cooper made his way to the plastic block, scavenged the area with his eyes quickly, dropped heavily into the block, and fell fast asleep.

Cooper woke up, seeing nothing at first. Day had turned to night. Cooper wasn't sure where he was, or how he got there. After shaking off the confounding remnants of sleep, he remembered everything again. He felt surprisingly refreshed. I must have slept for eight hours, he thought to himself. He felt rejuvenated, strength had returned to his constitution. He stretched out his legs, inhaled deeply, filling his chest with the mildly cool night air, and noticed his cough

had desisted. He grabbed his neck, took another

gluttonous breath, feeling the coarseness of his throat

had dissipated. He walked over to the water fountain

adjacent to the playground, took a few big sips,

walked back towards the block, and stopped abruptly.

Cooper froze like a man looking down over a

precipice, facing a potential free fall into oblivion.

There by the swing set, a dark figure, standing stolidly

silent, eerily complacent, and breathlessly patient

looked straight at Cooper with unflinching solemnity.

Cooper was overcome

by a quivering tremble that danced across his body

like the droplets from a melting ice cube. He couldn't

move, paralyzed by an overbearing, unreasonable

fear. The dark figure approached him, stepped into the light of the street lamp, and revealed a ghostly pale, translucent complexion that almost radiated against the glare of the lamp. Cooper couldn't make out anything but the face, the figure's body seemingly cloaked in some sort of garment. Two big, black eyes gushed forth from that pallid face, encompassing both a benevolent assurance, and a wickedly venomous seductive quality. The figure's glare steadied on Cooper. Nothing stirred, not a drop of a breeze.

"Hello Cooper," the figure spoke, in a low voice, emotionlessly. Cooper couldn't take his eyes off that cryptic figure. He didn't want to look at those eyes, but found that he couldn't turn away.

"It is you," Cooper said, feeling the paralysis

wane within his body, "but not you. You sound different."

"The circumstances are different," the figure said.

"What do you want?"

"It is not what I want," said the figure.

"I don't understand," said Cooper taking one step back.

"You were never meant to."

"Why did you terrorize me like that?"

"You will not find the answer satisfactory."

"There are a lot of things that I don't find satisfactory," Cooper said, remaining solidly planted.

"I don't expect this to be any different."

"It was an experiment," the figure said, revealing a molecule of a smirk, after what felt to Cooper like an interminable silence. Cooper felt submerged in a coldness that resonated to the very marrow of his bones.

After taking a few staggering steps back, Cooper said, "What the hell does that mean?"

"I tried to warn you Cooper," The figure said.

"Good god, what the hell are you telling me? Are we all just a bunch of silly, farcical pets that can be toyed with on a whim?" Cooper almost shrieked. "Impossible!"

"And if I would have said that you were

specially designated, would that have made a difference?" the figure spoke, closing the gap between them.

"Anything would have been better than being called a toy."

After a silence ensued the figure said, "You were given everything you needed Cooper."

"Something tells me not to believe you. Could you be deceiving me?" Cooper said, to himself, in a resigned manner, standing weaker than before.

"Thus, the nature of man," the figure spoke, taking his eyes off Cooper for the first time, looking down. "Filled to the brim with convictions about himself, and an ego that can never be severed. The mysteries beyond your personal reality deemed

irrelevant, and the scope of your conceptions minimal

at best."

"Then what is the damn point?" Cooper said.

"You're telling me it is all meaningless?"

"No."

"Then what? I demand an answer!"

The figure waited, with an implacable presence,

stemming from that chalk-white face. A few seconds

of silence ensued.

"Man is truly remarkable," the figure spoke, in a

tone more human now. "You cling to an irretrievable

truth to the very end. Even when being faced by the

very personification of it."

"So that's it," Cooper said, in a quiet manner. "I felt afraid at first, but now I feel a tremendous calm about everything." Cooper looked around, looked up at the night sky. Is this real? Cooper thought to himself. The figure slowly nodded, answering his thought. Cooper lowered his head. After a few moments he looked back at the figure, who resumed a penetrating gaze.

"I never meant to hurt Maggie," Cooper said. His hands shook violently, and the muscles in his chin convulsed.

"I know," the figure replied. "Are you ready to go?" the figure said after a few seconds.

"Is this how it is with everyone?" Cooper inquired.

"No."

"Where are you taking me," Cooper said, after the figure rested his palm on his shoulder leading him toward the open field.

"Everything in due course," the figure responded. They walked slowly, Cooper slightly in front of the figure, who moved his palm to the middle of Cooper's back. Cooper felt an immense force on his back, even though their pace was even, and unhurried.

"Will I be able to see Jonas there?" Cooper said, with watery eyes. The figure did not respond and they receded into the night.

◆

Stanley tip toed onto the playground as the stars dotted the midnight sky, with a half moon veiled behind a few faint clouds that looked like bars of oval soap connected at the hip. The large branches of the Walnut tree suspended lifelessly over the park, without a trace of wind, the only proof that oxygen was present founded in the heat Stanley felt on his upper lip from his exhaling nostrils. Placing his guitar case on the ground, he walked slowly around the swing set to the plastic block behind the bridge. Whispering softly, Stanley, said, "Cooper? Cooper?

You here?" He turned around, making a circular

motion with his body, looking all around the park.

"Cooper? Where are you?" he said a bit louder.

Suddenly the wind picked up, and a heavy gust

washed over Stanley's body dying down just as fast as

it came, reverting everything back to an icy stillness.

He looked up at the stars momentarily, walked back

towards the swings, unlocked his guitar case, took out

his guitar, sat in the swing, and sang.

Someday you'll find that the

world left you out

No true love, no nothing, just roaming about

Wild parties and people, and a cold heart within

And each time you're dancing, you're waltzing with sin

POETRY

Dead Hall Dance

Why does he look at me like that?

Those eyes consumed with alligator toenails

He wears the right clothes, his beard is meticulously
unkempt, He covets

the hallways with his unsavory lips

She looked irritated, a slight tremor in her chin, her
toes winking at me

We bartered words

Everything communicated through the hot breath of
empty space

Shrieks arose from his shoulder blades, freckle
spangled knuckles tap danced on

holey knees

The light burned, orchestrating the dance, the walls
assented forming the choir of

white that we placed on each other's tongues

She, a wordless window that severed the engagement

The music ceased in her, but the strings remained in
key

He kept on and on like savage rain, the pungent
fragrance of dead water fleeing

underneath

His eyebrows boxed, His nose the referee, Me with a
front row seat

I left before the bell rang

Befriending the Lemon

I once dealt with a brat *himself / herself.*

One whose breath was skinless, *life is meaningless / pointless.*

And could turn the sun into the moon. *made everything depressing*

One who dreamed the blue sky,

and contoured the purple valleys.

One who never rested, *concious always aware.*

Yet always brought fatigue. *& always tired.*

One who shot nails through graphite tombs,

And sulked naked on icy corner blocks.

One who soared with blooming tenure

And laid blank under balloonfish floors.

One who insisted the gray was black,

And turned everything to red.

One who ranted the mimetic binds,

And succumbed to nothing but transient whims.

One who feasted on the tight sail,

And rushed into the ghostly gale.

I once dealt with a brat

That cried when it was sunny,

And laughed at soggy clouds.

That saturated night with weeping, ~~filled the~~ ~~night crying~~

And coughed during the day.

That danced on graveyards,

And plugged the fireless entrance.

I once dealt with a brat

That flowered monstrous paranoia,

and gnawed the aging foundation.

That slurped soup, while sitting under the crown,

And pampered the denizens of faithless grounds.

I once dealt with a brat

Who lured my grip, seized my lip

Who tore the rainbow's chain asunder,

And revealed a world of colors sight unseen.

At last I put this brat to sleep,

And am withstanding its tantrums with every breath...

Song of Blue

Leaning on the wheel, feverish

amber glazed pine trees swayed like children of the earth

He bent his head out the window

trying to blanket his incomprehension around her perfectness

Silence fooled him dreamy resignation

Idealism swam freely in his chest

Sentimentality swelled his cheeks

The last stitch of light dissipated

It was time

he knew

They waited

patient as always

He sang to them

tongue dipped in ancient sadness

home

Sleep Well (Ode to Lorca)

He stands alone, feet torn by hungry sidewalks

Disentangled, disconsolate, disowned by the melting
faces kissing his shoulders

Like a torn rag from god's shawl, dancing unheeded,
breathless, eternally worn

Ravaged by images dripping off the metal torsos of
industrial nights

Seething with the blood of lightless valleys, swimming
with the stars in pools of lavender

Listening solemnly to the songs of weeping hillsides,
and the pounding silence of a golden desert

He stands alone

Where babies wail for the milk of dead kings, and
mothers walk slowly through forests of seared dollar
bills

With dark brows tattooed by the Spanish Sun, and
flesh borne from the roots of nameless sycamores

He stands alone

With language ripped from the belly of the Earth,
twirling, mincing, dancing on the tip of his mind like
drunken butterflies

With hurricanes of time's debris brushing against his
cobweb eyelashes, splattered against the walls of his
mossy temples

He stands alone

Fraught with lyrical moonshine drowned in the drunkard's plea, trembling with the choir of the immovable graves

Singing his song silently to the captives of the night, eating the bread hardened by the wails of sardine families penetrating steely silver rooftops with cracked aloofness

There he stands--> in between coffee tables, underneath winter blemished leaves, behind the bark of ancient elms, dreaming sleeplessly afloat the white wash of the impervious Atlantic, deep in the folds of a child's sock, laughing heartily on the fingernail of oblivion, stretching his limbs in the amber sky

There he sleeps—> on the backbone of the crescent moon, on the fire escapes of sweaty courthouses, amidst the mist gushing from the horses breath, inside the melody of the damned sparrow, alongside the silver blade of the unquenchable hunter, immersed in the rain of a summer night, in the puddle of that last sip of wine, underneath the feet of god in the womb of time

Sleep well...

ncomfortably in their

Discussing   f society, mindlessly
chattering about chem...   aste

Political stances dripping from their heavy tongue's

I am shooting hoops with old friends, bouncing the
basketball to my own rhythm

The summer bugs flying around my face, more
courageous than any great general

They buzz around my juicy head because they have to,
not because they have anything to gain, therefore they
are successful

I glide past the adults and head into the living room where the children are playing board games

Their laughter invites me in, their faces beam with encouragement

Their voices fly over the heavy air, carry more resonance with me

I take a load off in the easy chair and immediately feel at home

The exchange lifts me; the games more than I could ask for

I think to myself, "This is much more fun than going out to a stupid club or bar."

These kids have nothing to prove, they have nothing to hide

Their enjoyment comes naturally, their smiles are

unforced

I feel the adults looking at me with suspicious glances
from the patio

"What could a thirty year old gain from hanging out
with thirteen and ten year olds?" their looks tell me

Only God and I could answer that

And their too useless to explain anything to

I'll let him do the talking...

ESSAY

WHY I WRITE

Why do I want to be a writer? Who knows? Why does any man want to do anything at all? What makes a man want to gamble? What makes him want to study the essence of plants? The history of war? Where do all the multitudes of inclinations spawn from that are embedded in the hearts of men? I cant really explain it too clearly. I'm not sure that I should even attempt to. I only know that the desire to write struck me as does everything else, in a swooping moment, a flash across the eyes, a molecular jolt, if you will, and there is little to account for it and almost always arrives unplanned. But it's not as simple as that either. The moment a man realizes he is a writer is instantaneous, hits him right in the gut, but he has always been a writer, probably even before he was born. The recognition of this fact is the part that strikes him so seemingly swift. It can be compared to the sudden urge of wanting ice cream or a taste of some exotic food. Now, these desires may befall someone indeterminately and capriciously but the love of these things has, without too much debate, been stitched into his taste buds long ago. Although writing is much more important to me than the taste of rocky road, the persuasion of the two lies under the same roof. Well, actually that's not exactly right. Ice Cream is pretty serious business and certainly doesn't lack any significance at all, and, in most cases, takes precedence over everything. You see what I mean dear reader? This explanation stuff is pretty difficult to execute, especially when a man is trying to convey the understanding of his duty on this Earth.

I believe every man has a duty to fulfill and no duty surpasses the other in importance. That could be something like scratching the surface of meaning in a meaningless world. It all means nothing really, or at least means whatever the limits of your belief will make allowances for, and that doesn't bother me at all. I never understood the desire to grasp meaning at all costs and pursue it with so much energy and vigor. Seems like a waste and I can't afford to waste anything. I always liked there to be that mystique shrouding over things. I was comfortable with the accumulation of questions and the sparse answers in response. I accepted uncertainty and reveled in the endless maze of life- I never found any cheese and am not sure I really ever wanted to. Everything I did turned into this perpetual state of discovery. Once discovery was made then where do you go? Nowhere. You have to put it to rest and hop on another line. Writing was always to me this fantastic roadway to the gods. The journey of all journey's. I always felt like

I was on some wild escapade through unknown lands and uncharted waters, like Lewis and Clark, I was unveiling worlds that no one had ever seen before. I would jump on the path without a clue and somehow end up somewhere over the hills basking in the spectacle of man, the universe unfolding before my very eyes. I was very lucky because I wasn't living the experiences, the experiences were living me. I just happened to be around to check it all out, was invited to the big bash and I had to go whether I wanted to or not. Sometimes I wanted to simply take it easy and go off by myself somewhere and forget about man and all his achievements and tragedies. I had no choice however and I didn't mind that either.

Writing was also the only way, or one of the few ways, I could subdue my restlessness. I was always one of those who rocked a lot, fidgeted, twitched with a mounting energy inside that needed release. I would get bored too quickly at most activities and I found

that there was little I could do to suppress that

boredom and I tried a lot of things to get around it.

Not even the magical charm of a lovely woman could

keep my nerves at a standstill for too long a time.

Sooner or later I would be up and about again,

bouncing around, locomotives dashing through my

veins, with an urge to go, to leave, flee, and get out

there, be a part of something, anything, or aimlessly

meander, the point was to keep moving, keep

unveiling the world's secrets around you. A ceaseless,

enflamed, compulsion to cling to the coattails of

discovery. Like a shark, I needed to be moving all the

time or else. The very moment I felt like I had arrived

somewhere I would be assailed by a bizarre

uneasiness, and then in comes that old feeling

creeping up my back and into my neck, poking me,

nudging me, saying, "Hey you! Time to set off!" and I

was out there again in the twilight mayhem scouring, like a hunter that can't satisfy his hunger. There was never anything specific I was trying to discover, I was just oppressed with this vague, nameless ache to be out there under the sky before my fellow men and women. I wanted to taste everything, smell all the smells emanating from the Earth, feel the gleam of every star in my eyes, hear the song of every leaf that trembled, feel the soft thump of every woman's bosom when pressed against mine. I didn't want to miss anything, I mean ANYTHING, and I was driven to great depths of sorrow and exultancy by this incessant thorn pricking my soul, this immutable voice screeching in my ears. I was always in a perpetual state of rankled nerves, profound indecision, and utter vexation. I think I still am, but maybe not as much as when I was younger. You cant be in the red forever, the engine wont last as long.

I discovered writing somewhere along the way, discovered that writing was in me and that some form of writing was taking place in me somewhere all the time. I had the manuscripts tucked away in me, somewhere safe, ready to be transcribed at any moment I was able to stop time, for time is one of the great inhibitors. I needed to swallow up as much time as possible as I was out there like a ball of thunder soaking up all the nectar I could and then I would need to come home to the empty page and break every clock in sight. The important thing was to kill the awareness of time so I could write what was written in me thousands of years ago. Give time a taste of its own medicine, sort of slap it in the face with one hard smack, open up every mouth, every voice within me that had been hushed by the piles of minutes and hours. Writing allowed me to not only stop time but to stop thinking altogether and I was on autopilot; a succinct, high-powered, piston popper of a machine. Setting it down without any strain, effortless, fluid, like a swans neck I was graceful in my movements, and every contour of the page molded itself to my words. A nightingale never thinks about its song, whether or not it's the right tune, or if its appropriate or not, it just belts out the song with all its glory and blasts the night with a brilliant refrain that you had to listen to, it was impossible not to. I wanted to write like a nightingale, felt akin to its lonesome spirit. I didn't want to muddle my melody with my meddling thoughts. My thoughts were what shook me up, left me dangling on the line between here and nowhere. I never felt restless when I was writing and more than usually, I felt sleepy after a good, long session. I wonder if the nightingale ever felt sleepy after singing...

My roaming nature was a perfect accompaniment to being a writer. I became keen in my observations and hardly anything went unnoticed by my hungry eyes. I was telepathic, I could see into things with clarity and foresight. I was a trained marksman and my target was everything and everybody. I could hear the sound of a woman's voice and decipher exactly what kind of cigarettes she probably smoked, whose side she was on, where she bought her clothes, and what kind of thoughts swam in her head. I could look at a child sitting alone on the beach with head bent down and feel all the loneliness in the world. I could perceive events before they happened too. I was walking down the street one time in a street fare, people everywhere, swarms coming and going. I noticed one face that stood out above the rest. He was wearing nothing in particular that gave him away, nothing too outlandish, but his eyes were conveying everything going on inside him. I had a front row seat and couldn't wait till intermission. I turned to my friend and said, "Something is going to happen." She looked at me warily and shrugged off my warning. I could feel it though, like a hurricane rumbling in the distance. I kept my eye on that guy the whole time and when he passed us I turned around and he bashed some unsuspecting fellow with an empty bottle that came out of the inside of his jacket. The crowd parted with fear and screams were heard. The instigator spat on the poor man lying on the floor and then ran off, security hot on his trail. The fare was pretty much broken up after that and everybody started to make way for their homes, and the victim was being looked after by paramedics. My friend took me aside and astonishingly questioned me as to how I knew "something" was going to happen. I couldn't explain it too well, just told her that I could see it somehow clear in my head, something in the guy's face struck me cold, and I felt a chill all over. I couldn't avoid him and It was like his will anchored itself in my flesh and I was hooked with nowhere to go. This too had been placed in me long before I had the power of memory.

I was intrigued by everything. The whole spectrum of life was a magnificent ray beamed across my body and I never looked for any shade. I wanted to bury myself in the sand, feel the beating hum-drum of life, synchronize myself with the rhythm of the planets. I was never at home and I worried my folks till they were gray in the head. I couldn't stand enclosed spaces, took the stairs instead of the elevator, and preferred windows over doors. I didn't want anything to block my path, or to hinder my sight. There wasn't a molecule of air that I didn't milk for all its worth. My lungs were well fed every day and were as strong as a thoroughbreds. I smoked all types of smoke and ate all sorts of treats and still had enough left in the chest to run across the plains and tumble with the ramblers, chase down fireflies and howl with the wolves.

I never practiced patience, or at least I was all too impatient to get what I was thirsting for. There was never enough for me and I didn't see the point in waiting around. Wait around for what? I mean I wasn't at all ambitious, at least not in the strictest definition. I was ambitious to *live* and be lived but there wasn't any desire to climb any ladders, or look out at tall buildings, gain recognition from others, or to swindle the great monument of commerce. My ambitions were bigger than that. I never thought of having goals, the thought struck me violently and I wanted to spit them out of my head immediately. Goals? Never had any, or If I did they were never something thought out and long term. I absorbed everything as it came, was privy to the futility of making order out of the chaos. The idea of planning things out and just following them religiously was, to me, like mocking the gods, giving yourself too much credit. Things never worked out the way you wanted them to. They only worked in a universal kind of way, with no consideration for your petty vanity but with grave consideration for your placement. This was all fine with me as well, I preferred it that way. There really was no alternative.

I knew I wanted to do *something*, but I never gave it a shape, or color. I didn't feel I had to. It changed faces constantly, wouldn't let me get too comfortable with just one. If I was a sketch artist I would have to draw something with a thousand heads. My something was everything wrapped around a whole lot of nothing. I wanted to become a creator of sorts, but I didn't realize at the time that there wasn't a gesture gestured or a step stepped that was devoid of creativity. A creator creates even when he thinks he is not. He can't help but create; it would be like water being wet only part of the time. When I was with my friends and I was in one of my ridiculous moods, I would create laughter. When I felt like being more solemn I would sing an old Elizabethan ballad and move myself into moving others with the heroic, magical tale on my six string guitar and then receive laughter for the foolish way I was being so solemn; nobody could laugh at me the way I could laugh at myself. I always got the biggest kick out of everything, people were always accusing me of laughing too much. In conversations a creator is like no other, whipping off words and phrases with a gilded tongue, using terms no other has ever uttered. Talking like the sun, blasting people with color of personality and action. A creator walks like no other as well using his feet in a new way, peculiar to those with dullness of spirit, alluring to those who recognize his way of taking himself lightly. A creator takes everything lightly for the sheer reason he takes everything so severely. He sees the humor in everything and laughs at no one. He laughs at the way everything seems to go, the progression of this carnival called life. He even laughs at death, the ultimate joke on mankind. He thinks he has done some work or other that he foolishly calls his masterpiece, but he is mistaken. His entire existence is his masterpiece; a walking, talking, eating, sleeping, crying, dying masterpiece. It means nothing yet it means *something*. The something always outweighs the nothing, but you can't get around either one of them without running into the other. Why do I write? I have no idea, but I can't stop...

Dr. Kelly Buffone

38030451R00144

Made in the USA
San Bernardino, CA
29 August 2016